C0-ANT-194

THE NEW IMPERIALISM

The
New Imperialism

A BACKGROUND BOOK

Hugh Seton-Watson

THE BODLEY HEAD

LONDON SYDNEY

TORONTO

LIBRARY
FLORIDA STATE UNIVERSITY
TALLAHASSEE, FLORIDA

© Hugh Seton-Watson 1961, 1971
ISBN 0 370 10277 0
ISBN 0 370 01366 2 (paperback)
Printed and bound in Great Britain for
THE BODLEY HEAD LTD
9 Bow Street, London WC2
by William Clowes and Sons Ltd, Beccles
Set in Linotype Baskerville
First published 1961
New edition 1971

CONTENTS

1

What is Imperialism?

THE word 'imperialism' has been variously interpreted in a vast literature, both polemical and scientific. No definition has yet been universally accepted, and this is no place to make a new attempt. It is, however, necessary to explain in general terms how imperialism will be understood in the following pages.

The irreducible core of meaning in the word is domination by persons of one nation over another nation. This domination may result from the deliberate decision of a government, as when the Ottoman rulers decided to conquer the Balkan Peninsula and Constantinople. It may be the work of adventurers who owe allegiance to a distant sovereign, and place their conquests under his authority: examples are the foundation of the colony of Virginia, or the conquest of Mexico by Cortes. Sometimes a whole nation, recognising no metropolitan ruler, moves into new lands and conquers its inhabitants: there are many examples in the history of Central Asia, and the case of the Voortrekkers in South Africa is a modern example. A third type of situation arises when the conquerors repudiate their metropolitan ruler, like the North and South American colonists, who did not cease to be conquerors of the indigenous Indians by the mere fact that they proclaimed lofty principles of liberty for themselves.

The result of conquests may be extermination of the original population, or the exploitation of its labour by the conqueror. Most imperial conquests show a combination, in widely varying proportions, of these two processes.

The motives of conquest have been very diverse. The simplest is loot, in the form of tangible material wealth and slaves. In the expansion of Europe in the eighteenth and nineteenth centuries perhaps the most frequent aim was trade, whether by sea or land. Regular trade required security of access to markets, of transport routes and of stocks of goods. Security required stable laws and their efficient enforcement. Disputes about such matters led to the seizure of territory piecemeal, ending in the overthrow of governments and the annexation of territories. At the end of the nineteenth century the search for raw materials and minerals was sometimes a motive of conquest. But conquest has often had motives that were not material. The result may have been still more disagreeable for the conquered, but the difference is still real. Emigrants seeking liberty of conscience in a new land played a great part in the colonisation of North America. Obvious examples of missionary conquest—designed to impose the truth by force on the heathen—are the Arab conquests of the seventh and eighth centuries and the Spanish conquest of a large part of South America. Another variation is armed intervention to end social abuses. The British annexation of a large part·of East Africa was inspired by the desire to suppress Arab slave-trading.

Domination can, however, be secured without formal imposition of foreign rule. The Ottoman Empire and China in the nineteenth century were forced to give commercial privileges to European traders, who enjoyed extra-territorial legal status. Though they exercised no formal sovereignty, they were a class privileged above all Ottoman or Chinese subjects, and often displayed towards the host nation an arrogance which was bitterly, if at first silently, resented.

The English economist Hobson, in his work *Imperialism*, published in 1902, emphasised the connection between capitalism and imperialism. This aspect was developed further by the Marxists Roza Luxemburg, Rudolf Hilferding and Vladimir Lenin. No serious student can deny that the contribution of the Marxist school to the problem is of great value. But contemporary communist orthodoxy claims more than this. It claims that Lenin has given a complete scientific analysis and definition of imperialism. Imperialism

8

is due to capitalism, and when capitalism is removed, by the abolition of private property over the means of production, distribution and exchange, imperialism must cease to exist. There can be no imperialism without private capital, no imperialism under socialism.

This is far too narrow a conception of imperialism. There was domination and exploitation of one nation by another before the age of private capitalism, and there is such domination in countries where there is no private capitalism. In the Soviet Union private capital is insignificant, and the means of production are in the hands of the state. But the Soviet government exercises direct domination over about 90,000,000 non-Russian subjects, and indirectly rules a further 90,000,000 persons in European satellite states and about 10,000,000 in Asian satellite states.

The old imperialism of the European empires, established under private capitalism, is rapidly disappearing from the face of the earth. Direct rule by Europeans over non-Europeans still exists in a large part of Southern Africa (whether by a metropolitan government or, as in the Union, by a government whose sole seat of power is in Africa), and in a few places in Asia and in the Pacific. It can also be argued that in some South American states the power exercised by foreign capital amounts to indirect imperialism. But, in contrast to the declining power of European Colonial Powers and of North American business, the new imperialism of the Soviet Union is vigorous, has enormously expanded its territory since 1945, and aims at further expansion. It has a double origin. On the one hand the Soviet government inherited the Russian Empire, half of whose subjects were non-Russians conquered by the Tsars. On the other hand the Soviet government is controlled by the Communist Party, inspired by a missionary ideology, which it is its duty to impose, by whatever means are expedient, whenever opportunity is offered, on those nations which have not yet accepted the communist faith or communist institutions.

In the following pages we shall consider the historical record of Soviet imperialism, beginning with the heritage of the old Russian Empire and then considering the new aims and new methods which resulted from the Bolshevik (Communist) revolution and from the victory of the Soviet Union in the Second World War.

2

The Russian Empire

EUROPEAN Russia is a land without natural frontiers, a
great plain divided into two main regions, the forest and the
steppe, and crossed by great rivers, of which the greatest
are the Dniepr and the Volga. In this area various states
succeeded each other in ancient times, established and
destroyed, like other states elsewhere, by force. The first
Russian state, inhabited by people speaking a Slav speech
that is the prototype of the modern Russian language, was
created in the ninth century or earlier, on the border between forest and steppe, around the valley of the Dniepr.
Its capital was at Kiev, and its rulers adopted Christianity
in 988. It expanded to the north and east, into the forests,
whose original Finnish inhabitants were destroyed or fled
or adopted the Russian language and the Christian religion.
Though torn by the quarrels of individual princes, and har-
ried by the raids of nomadic tribes which entered the steppe
from the east, the Kiev state achieved a considerable civilisation, influenced mainly by Byzantium, and maintained
diplomatic and commercial relations with the medieval
monarchies of Europe.

Between 1236 and 1240 the Kiev state was destroyed by the
Mongol prince Batu, a grandson of the great conqueror
Djinghiz Khan. The Russian princes became tributaries of
a new state, the Golden Horde, whose capital was at Saray
on the lower Volga. The khans of the Golden Horde were
the heirs of the Mongol conquerors, but the people were
not Mongols but Tatars, speaking a language closely related
to Turkish. In the fourteenth century the Tatar rulers
adopted Islam as their religion. During the fourteenth and
fifteenth centuries one of the Russian principalities, based

11

on the city of Moscow, was able, with strong support from the Orthodox Church, to achieve supremacy over the other Russian principalities, and then to assert its independence of the Tatar khans. The latter task was made easier by the divisions within the Tatar camp. The Golden Horde split into three states, based respectively on Kazan, on the middle Volga, on Astrakhan, at the mouth of the Volga, and on the Crimean Peninsula. The Tsar of Muscovy, Ivan IV ('the Terrible'), conquered Kazan in 1552 and Astrakhan in 1556.

Whether the expansion of Muscovy to the Volga valley was 'liberation' or 'imperialism' depends on the point of view of the observer. The Kiev state had included part of the valley, but this was of course the result of earlier conquest. The Tatars had seized it by conquest, and were now subdued by the same means. But though Russian nobles and peasants colonised the area from the sixteenth century onwards, great numbers of Tatars remained, in addition to smaller language groups which were neither Russian nor Tatar, and some of which were neither Christian nor Moslem. In Russian literature and folklore the Volga is the great 'Russian river', but it is equally possible to argue that right up to the end of the nineteenth century it remained, in population, a Tatar, that is, a Turkish river.

The relation of Muscovy to the Tatars is not unlike that of Castile to the Moors. The Visigothic kingdom of Spain was built by conquest, by an 'imperialism' whose victim was the Roman Empire. The Visigoths were conquered by the Arabs, who for at least five centuries maintained a civilisation of great distinction on Spanish soil. To Christian historians, the expansion of the small northern kingdoms at the expense of the Moors was the *Reconquista*, the liberation of Spain. But to the Moslems it was aggression by the northern barbarians. Both in Russia and in Spain the wars of reconquest had the character of a crusade. Religious fervour on both sides brought an additional element of bitterness and cruelty.

In the case of Russia the process did not end with the

conquest of the Volga valley. The Crimean Tatars remained a formidable power for another two hundred years. They were backed by the greatest Islamic state, the Ottoman Empire, whose vassals they became in 1475. The Ottoman Empire, with its capital in the sacred city of Orthodox Christianity, Constantinople, held all the shores of the Black Sea, and barred the access of Muscovy to the Mediterranean world. Though Peter the Great (1689–1725) had some successes in war against Crimea and the Ottoman Empire, it was not until 1783 that the Crimean peninsula was finally annexed to Russia.

* * *

The distinction between Europe and Asia is artificial in Russian geography, and makes no sense in Russian history. The Ural mountains are not a serious physical barrier. The essence of the eastward expansion of the Russian state is the conflict between a Christian and a Moslem culture, and this was fought along the Volga and in the Black Sea steppes, both of which lie within the geographical area known as Europe. But Ivan IV's conquest of Kazan and Astrakhan made it possible for adventurous Russians to travel east. During the seventeenth century Russians colonised Siberia, and reached the river Amur in the Far East. Here was signed in 1689 the Treaty of Nerchinsk with China, which fixed the Russian Empire's border for nearly two centuries. In the eighteenth century Russian sovereignty was established in the peninsula of Kamchatka, and Russian explorers made contact with the people of the Kurile Islands. At the end of the century there were Russian settlements in Alaska.

If Spanish history offers a parallel to Moscow's wars with the Tatars, the colonisation of Siberia recalls that of North America. Both these vast areas were sparsely populated. The Siberian peoples were as primitive as the Red Indians, and as ruthlessly exterminated. If the Russian colonists were cruel, they had, like their American equivalents, the courage and the individual enterprise of the pioneer. Among them were many who were escaping from serfdom, or from religious persecution: in this too there is a striking resemblance to the American case. The Americans were, however, more fortunate in being separated from Europe by the ocean. When the time came, the Americans of north and south could break away from England and Spain. But continuous land communication favoured the Russian autocracy. In the end the government of St. Petersburg caught up with the rugged individualists of Siberia. Even so, they were able, right up to 1917, to preserve greater freedom, and a more self-reliant spirit, than any other subjects of the Tsars.

* * *

It was not only in the east and south that Muscovy expanded. During Russia's subjection to the Tatars, its western borderlands, including Kiev itself, had been conquered by the pagan rulers of Lithuania, which was later united with Poland. In the sixteenth and seventeenth centuries Poland was one of the Great Powers of Europe, and in frequent conflict with Muscovy. The territorial ambitions of the rulers were embittered by religious hatred, for Poland was considered the champion of Catholicism while the Tsars of Muscovy claimed to be the heirs of the Byzantine Emperors as defenders of the only true faith.

The struggle between Muscovy and Poland for the Ukraine can perhaps be compared with the struggle between France and the Holy Roman Empire for control of Burgundy, Lorraine and the Low Countries. Just as Dutchmen and Lorrainers were neither French nor German, so were Ukrainians and White Russians neither Poles nor Russians. *Ukraina* means 'the border'. This was in fact a no-man's-land between Poland, Muscovy, Crimea and Moldavia. In these sparsely populated steppes runaway serfs from both Poland and Russia sought escape from their masters. Around the rapids of the Dniepr a community of warriors, the Zaporozhian Cossacks, established a military power of their own, with a primitive social and political organisation, recognising no ruler as their lord and conducting war or diplomacy with the neighbouring states. In the mid-seventeenth century the people of the east bank of the Dniepr revolted against Poland under a great leader Bohdan Chmielnicki. In 1654, hard pressed by the Poles, Chmielnicki made an agreement with the Tsar of Muscovy, the Treaty of Pereyaslavl. This has been variously interpreted as an alliance between two states, a personal union between two states, or the simple submission of Orthodox Russians to the Russian Tsar. In practice, for the next fifty years the Cossacks of the east bank elected their own chieftain, the Hetman, who recognised the Tsar as his sovereign but exercised powers little less than those of an independent ruler. During the war between Peter the Great and Charles XII of Sweden, in 1709, the Hetman Isaac Mazeppa took the Swedish side. After his victory, Peter deprived the Cossacks of their autonomy. The east-bank Ukraine was simply incorporated in the Russian Empire, administered by officials appointed by the Tsar. At the end of the century, by the three Partitions of Poland (1772, 1793 and 1795) the rest of the borderlands was annexed to Russia.

These conquests had added the Ukraine to Russia. But who were its people? The traditional distinction was between Catholics and Orthodox. Under Polish rule, the landowners and officials had been Catholics and Poles, while most of the peasants were Orthodox. The latter were generally known as 'Little Russians'. They spoke dialects different from the 'Great Russian' language of Muscovy. Their social institutions were also distinct from those of central Russia: in particular they lacked the village commune which was the centre of Russian peasant society. Their legal and cultural traditions were Western, with Polish influence predominant. A minority of them belonged to the Uniate Church, a separate branch of Catholicism set up in 1595 with the aim of winning Russians from Orthodoxy to Rome, but which in reality had the effect of differentiating its members from both Poles and Russians. The people of the Ukraine considered themselves different from those of Muscovy, whom they called *moskaly*, and whose authority they resented, even if they preferred it on the whole to that of Poland. During the eighteenth century, as the Russian armies drove back the Tatars and finally annexed the Crimea, the almost empty steppes began to fill up with people from the formerly Polish lands. Thus by the end of the century the whole southern part of the Russian Empire in Europe was inhabited by people of Little Russian speech.

It is an anachronism to speak of a Ukrainian nation at that time. But during the nineteenth century a nation was formed. There appeared a small educated class which, while knowing the Russian language, was proud of its own speech, and sought to form from the Little Russian dialects a literary Ukrainian language. The man who contributed most to this end was the great poet Taras Shevchenko (1812–1861), who was also a revolutionary democrat. Once a Ukrainian literary language had taken shape, it became the point of crystallisation for the Ukrainian sense of identity and of difference from Russia. The social and cultural differences reinforced the linguistic difference, and a Ukrainian consciousness was born. The development of Ukrainian nationalism was also helped by the fact that a considerable Ukrainian community, living in eastern Galicia, had been annexed by Austria in the Partitions of Poland. In this western portion of the Ukraine the Uniate Church was stronger than the Orthodox, and became the stronghold of a Ukrainian nationalism which was directed both against Poles and against Russians. There were also Ukrainians in the north of Bukovina, a province annexed by Austria from the Ottoman Empire in 1775, and in Ruthenia, the north-eastern corner of the Kingdom of Hungary.

* * *

The eighteenth century saw the destruction of the Polish state, which was divided between its three greedy neighbours, Russia, Austria and Prussia. By these Partitions, the last of which was in 1795, Russia received not only the greater part of the Ukraine, but also the more northerly portion of the borderlands, known as White Russia. Here too the ruling class and landowners had long been Polish, but the peasants spoke a number of dialects generally known as White Russian. By religion they were partly Catholic, partly Uniate and partly Orthodox. Like the Ukraine, White Russia was a part of 'the Russian Land' in the sense that it had belonged to the Kiev state before the Mongol and Lithuanian conquests. Like the Ukrainians, the White Russians had different traditions and outlook from those of Muscovy. During the late nineteenth century there was a movement for the formation of a White Russian literary language, and the first beginnings of White Russian nationalism appeared. Both were much less developed than the similar trends in the Ukraine.

Under the Partitions considerable numbers of Poles were incorporated in the Russian Empire. In 1815, on the defeat of Napoleon, Russia still further extended her possessions in Poland. The 1815 settlement, which ought to be known as the Fourth Partition of Poland, set up a rump Kingdom of Poland to be united with Russia only through its ruler, Alexander I, who was to be Emperor of Russia and King of Poland. This personal union did not work very well, as neither side was willing to respect the rights of the other. In 1830 the Poles rebelled against Russia, and were defeated after a year's war. After this they lost most of their autonomy. In 1863 they again rebelled, and were again defeated. Thus from 1830 until 1917 the greater part of the Polish nation, in the narrowest sense (Polish-speaking Catholics) were conquered subjects of the Tsar.

To the north of White Russia the Partitions of Poland had given Russia the homeland of the small Catholic Lithuanian people. (A distinction must be made between Lithuania in this narrower ethnic sense and Lithuania in the wider historical sense, which includes a large part of eastern Poland and the Ukraine and most of White Russia.) North of Lithuania were the three principalities of Kurland, Livonia and Estland, in which the landowning and commercial classes were Germans and the peasants Latvians and

Esthonians. All three national groups were Protestant by religion. These territories were annexed by Russia during the eighteenth century.

* * *

To the south of the Ukraine lay the territories ruled since the fifteenth century by the Ottoman Turks. The nearest of these to Russia was Moldavia, the majority of whose people were Roumanians, Orthodox Christians by religion but speaking a language of their own which is predominantly Latin with a large admixture of Slav words. In several wars against Turkey in the eighteenth and nineteenth centuries Russian armies had occupied Moldavia, and the second Roumanian principality of Wallachia which lay between it and the Danube. To annex these lands was for long the aim of Russian policy. But this aim was not achieved. The most that could be done was to annex the eastern half of Moldavia, lying between the rivers Dniestr and Prut, which became Russian in 1812, and was given the name of Bessarabia. Its population was in majority Roumanian. In the mid-nineteenth century the rest of Moldavia was combined with Wallachia to form the Principality, later the independent kingdom, of Roumania, which thus escaped subjection to Russia.

* * *

In the far north of European Russia the neighbour was Sweden, which had for centuries included Finland. Several wars were fought between Russia and Sweden on Finnish soil. After its brief period as a conquering military power in the seventeenth century, Sweden rapidly declined. In the war of 1808–1809 Russian armies overran Finland. Alexander I decided to become Grand Duke of Finland, leaving the Grand Duchy in possession of its own legal system and political institutions and quite separate from Russia. This personal union, unlike that of Poland with Russia from 1815 to 1830, worked well until the end of the century.

In the south-east, after the capture of Astrakhan in 1556,

Muscovy came into contact with the peoples of the Caucasus. The Kabardins and Ossetins, occupying the central portion of the long west-to-east mountain barrier, became associated with the Russians. The Circassians, inhabiting the western part of the range and the slopes descending to the Black Sea, were hostile to Russia, and looked for protection to Turkey across the sea. At the eastern end of the range, a strip of low land along the Caspian Sea gave easy access in the direction of Persia. Behind this strip, in the mountains of the eastern part of the Caucasus, the Chechens and the peoples of Daghestan fiercely defended their independence against any invader.

Beyond the main Caucasus range lie two large river basins, separated from each other by the watershed of the Little Caucasus range and facing respectively to the Black Sea and the Caspian, and thus militarily vulnerable respectively to Turkey and to Persia. This is the homeland of the Georgian people, Christian by religion since the fourth century and speaking a language completely different from that of its neighbours. The land closest to the Caspian had however been conquered from the Georgians in the eighth century by the Arab Moslem invasions, and was settled some time later by Turks who belonged, like the Persians who were their rulers, to the Shia branch of Islam. They are known as the Azeri Turks, and their country is called Azerbaidjan. Beyond Georgia and Azerbaidjan was the homeland of the Armenians, a Christian people with a history still older than the Georgians, who by the end of the sixteenth century had been divided between the Ottoman and Persian empires, by far the larger part in the former.

During the eighteenth century Russia fought several wars against Persia, in which the Georgians were her allies. In 1783 the chief kingdom of Georgia placed itself under the protectorate of Russia, and in 1801 its king George XIII asked that it should be directly annexed. Other Georgian principalities had to be conquered by Russian arms. In 1813 Persia surrendered half of Azerbaidjan, including the peninsula of Baku, to Russia. In 1828 Persia further

19

surrendered her portion of Armenia. The frontier between Russia and Turkey in Transcaucasia changed several times as a result of the varying fortunes of Russo-Turkish wars, but the districts affected were not large. The bulk of the Armenian people, which would have liked to be annexed by Russia, remained in Turkey. Throughout the first half of the nineteenth century there was fierce resistance to Russia from the peoples of the west and east ends of the Caucasus range. The Chechens were not finally subdued until 1859, the Circassians until 1864.

*   *   *

South of the area of Russian colonisation in Siberia were the so-called Kirgiz steppes (known to-day as Kazakhstan). These gradually came under Russian sovereignty during the eighteenth and nineteenth centuries. Their people were nomadic herdsmen, organised in tribes or 'hordes'. South of the steppes were the settled areas of Turkestan, with an agricultural civilisation and an ancient culture, grouped round the valleys of the Oxus (Amur-Darya) and Jaxartes (Syr-Darya) and containing such famous cities as Samarkand and Bokhara. Relations between Russia and the rulers of these territories were bad. Subjects of the khans of Bokhara, Khiva or Kokand made raids on Russian territory, or robbed or captured Russian subjects—in many cases Tatar merchants from the Volga valley. Continual minor incidents were a source of annoyance to the Russian government. Russian and Tatar business-men hoped for commercial advantages if Turkestan were brought under Russian rule. Local Russian military commanders hoped for glory and promotion. In fact the same combination of factors operated as on the borders of the British and French empires, in India or Indo-China or North Africa. In the 1860's the Russian government decided to annex Turkestan. In a circular note to other European governments of 1864, the Russian Foreign Minister justified this action by the need to ensure the security of Russia's boundaries. He argued that the experience of Britain and the United States showed that when a civilised state comes into contact with barbarous peoples it is inevitable that the civilising power, in order to protect its subjects and suppress raiding, should constantly expand its boundary. This argument was considered perfectly reasonable by the Great Powers of the time, and indeed entirely conformed to their own practice. In 1865 the Russians took Tashkent, which became the capital of their Central Asian territories. In 1873, after a short military campaign, they imposed on the khans of Khiva and Bokhara treaties which took territory and financial indemnities from them and placed the remnant of their lands under Russian protectorate. In 1876 the khanate of Kokand was incorporated in the Russian Empire. The conquests were completed between 1881 and 1884 by some bitter fighting against the Turkmens, whose land lay between the Oxus, the Caspian and the Persian frontier.

* * *

In the Far East Russia made substantial gains in the same period. Profiting from a war between China and the Western Powers, the Russian government offered its 'mediation' to the Chinese, and extracted, by the Treaty of Aigun of May 1858, a triangular area between the lower Amur, its junction with the Ussuri and the Pacific coast. Two years later, when China was again attacked by Britain and France, the Russians obtained, by the Treaty of Peking, a further strip between the Ussuri and the ocean, at the southernmost point of which they founded the port of Vladivostok. In 1875 a Russo-Japanese treaty ensured Russian possession of the whole island of Sakhalin in exchange for Japanese annexation of the Kurile archipelago. In the 1890's Russia pursued a vigorous policy of expansion in the Far East, whose aim was not so much to acquire territory as to obtain vast economic concessions in the north and political control over the Chinese government in Peking. With the help of French capital, Russia obtained first the Chinese Eastern Railway, crossing Manchuria from west to east, and then the South Manchurian Railway, extending from Harbin on the CER down to the Yellow Sea. At the same time Russia obtained a lease of the Liaotung Peninsula, with the naval base of Port Arthur and the commercial port of Dairen. Not content with all this, the Russian government proposed also to have a dominant influence in Korea. All attempts by the Japanese to strike a bargain with Russia on zones of influence were refused by the Russians. The result of Russian intransigence was the Russo-Japanese War of 1904–1905, which was won by Japan. In the subsequent peace settlement Russia had to give up the Liaotung Peninsula, the SMR and half Sakhalin, but retained the CER. In the last decade before the First World War the Russian and Japanese governments co-operated, at the expense of China and of the European Powers and the United States. Southern Manchuria and Korea were the Japanese sphere, while Russia was supreme in northern Manchuria and in Mongolia, where the genuine desire of the Mongols to escape from Chinese domination was exploited by the Russian government to impose an effective Russian protectorate.

Thus in four hundred years from the repudiation of Tatar suzerainty, the principality of Muscovy had grown into the vast Russian Empire. The geographical scale of the expansion is without parallel, but the methods are in no way unique. Every type of expansion and 'imperialism' known in the history of European and American states can be found in that of Russia. The Russian record is neither better nor worse than the others. Russian expansion in the Volga valley has its parallel in the Spanish *reconquista*, the absorption of the Ukraine in the French absorption of Burgundy and Lorraine, the colonisation of Siberia in the colonisation of North America, the subjection of the Caucasus in the English subjection of the Scottish Highlands, the annexation of Central Asia in the creation of the British and French empires, Russian imperialism in the Far East in the aggressions of other European imperial powers against China. Indeed the Russo-Japanese War shares with the Anglo-Boer war the distinction of more nearly approaching the Marxist model of an imperialist war undertaken for economic motives than any other examples in history.

The Russian record is as imperialist as that of any other great nation. Nevertheless Russian writers, from the Slavophiles of the mid-nineteenth century to the post-war Soviet historians, have frequently maintained that Russians are a people in some way incapable of aggression, and that the non-Russian peoples in some way 'voluntarily united with' Russia. There is also a widespread belief, especially strong among some Asian and African nationalists, that because Russian conquests were all over land, not over sea, they were somehow 'less imperialistic' than those of the European Atlantic nations.

*　　*　　*

The government of the Russian Empire was based on the principle of autocracy. All Russian subjects owed allegiance to the Tsar, who was responsible only to God. Provided that they loyally obeyed him, they enjoyed his protection regardless of whether they were Russian by speech or religion.

The administration of the Empire was highly centralised, and throughout the nineteenth century the tendency was to make it more uniform. At the beginning of the century the Baltic provinces were administered according to their traditional German laws, in the Ukraine many Polish laws were in force, and in the territories recently conquered from the Crimean Tatars, the Turks or the Caucasian peoples new administrations had to be created in which local traditions and Russian needs were balanced against each other. In Central Asia in the second half of the century Moslem traditional laws and customs were largely left in operation. However, there was a definite and growing belief in St. Petersburg that everything should conform to a general pattern. It should not be forgotten that in Europe in the eighteenth and nineteenth centuries centralism was usually considered to be progressive. It had been the practice not only of militarist Prussia and absolutist Austria but also of revolutionary France. Regional autonomies, or 'particularism', were thought to be reactionary. The obvious case was the Vendée in the age of the French Revolution. Thus not only monarchs and bureaucrats, but also liberals and even socialists, in Russia as well as in Europe, were impatient of local traditions and claims to self-government. But centralism was considered not as directed against the interests of the smaller peoples in the interest of the larger nations: rather it was thought to be a guarantee of better government for all.

Another important consideration in Russia was the military security of the frontiers. In the Lithuanian borderlands Poles were regarded as potentially disloyal, and Russians or even Germans were preferred both as officials and as owners of land. In the North Caucasus Russian Cossacks were given land along the Terek river as a bulwark against raiding tribes. In Transcaucasia there was on the whole a preference for Christian Armenians over Moslem Azeri Turks. Towards the end of the century the Russian government, which had previously considered the Baltic Germans to be some of its most loyal subjects, began to distrust them, and to seek ways of diminishing German influence in these maritime provinces, whose strategic importance was obvious in the event of war with the growing German Empire.

* * *

The Russian Tsar was the Emperor of all his subjects, but he was also a defender of the Orthodox Church. Those of his subjects who were Orthodox were 'more equal than the others'. After the fall of Kazan and Astrakhan to Ivan the Terrible, the Tatars of the Volga valley were subjected to proselytism and persecution by the Orthodox Church. This was stopped by the Empress Catherine II in the late eighteenth century, and in 1788 a Moslem Ecclesiastical Administration was created, under a *mufti* who resided in Orenburg, and in later years in Ufa. However, in the nineteenth century Orthodox missionaries still sought to convert Moslems, while the conversion of Orthodox Christians to another faith was prohibited by law. There was also keen rivalry between Orthodox and Moslems for converting the still pagan peoples that lived along the Volga or to the east of it (Udmurts, Cheremiss, Chuvash and others). The struggle between the missionaries of the two religions was also a struggle between national cultures and languages. One side wished to make these people not only Christians but Russians, the other to make them not only Moslems but Tatars. It is thus possible to speak not only of Russian cultural imperialism, but also of a Tatar cultural imperialism within the Russian Empire.

The Russian Orthodox Church was active not only against Islam but also against other Christian churches. The main enemy was Catholicism, embodied by the Polish element in the Lithuanian borderlands. The Orthodox Church used, and was used by, the state authorities in its fight against the Poles. The Uniate Church was abolished in Lithuania in 1839 and in the Ukrainian district of Kholm in 1875, its members being 'received back' into the Orthodox Church. In the Baltic provinces in the 1840's some thousands of Latvians and Estonians were converted from Protestantism to Orthodoxy, and in the 1880's a new campaign of proselytism was attempted, this time with less success. The Russian Orthodox hierarchy also did its best to bring under its control the separate Orthodox Church of Georgia, and encouraged the secular authorities to meddle with the internal organisation of the Gregorian Church in Armenia. It should be noted that the Orthodox Church itself had been subjected to strict control by the secular hierarchy since the time of Peter the Great, who established the Holy Synod, directed by a lay official, the Chief Procurator. Thus it is difficult to distinguish between the policy of the Church and the State. It can be said that the first three emperors of the nineteenth century tended rather to restrain than to encourage the proselytising action of the Church (with the exception of its action against the Poles). The last two emperors, however, Alexander III (1881–1894) and Nicholas II (1894–1917) identified themselves with the Church's intolerant policy.

Until the end of the nineteenth century the Russian Empire was an overwhelmingly agrarian country. Thus the occupation of Russians and non-Russians alike was agriculture. The original lands of the Principality of Muscovy were not greatly favoured by climate or soil. The forests, however, provided timber and furs, which were successfully exported, especially to England. Valuable export crops of northern and central Russia were flax and hemp. It was only as Muscovy expanded to the east and south, to the Volga, Crimea and Ukraine, that it acquired immensely rich grain-bearing lands. It would, however, be unfair to suggest that the Russians robbed the Tatars and the Cossacks of their grain. The truth is that until Russian rule became firmly established in these lands very little grain was produced. Southern Russia was the home of nomads and raiders, with few settled farmers. Only in the nineteenth century did the famous black soil yield its rich crops, while the building of railways made it possible for them to be carried from the Black Sea ports to the markets of Europe. For this the governments and ruling class of Russia must take the credit. Nevertheless it remains a fact that a very large part of the grain output of Russia came from lands the majority of whose population was not Russian, but Ukrainian or Tatar. Another important crop, beet, on which the sugar industry of the Empire was based at the end of the century, was principally grown in the area west of Kiev, by Ukrainian not Russian farmers. At the beginning of the twentieth century the Empire began to be a considerable producer of cotton, grown in its newly conquered possessions in Central Asia. The deliberate encouragement to the farmers of Turkestan to concentrate on cotton can be compared with the encouragement by the British authorities to the farmers of Egypt. The aim was the same—to supply the metropolitan country with a large and reliable supply of raw material for its textile industry. The Moscow region on the eve of the First World War received more than half its raw cotton from Central Asia.

The mineral wealth of the Empire also came largely

from areas of non-Russian population. The iron mines of the Urals (inhabited by Tatars or by minor primitive peoples) were developed in the eighteenth century, when Russia was one of the major exporters of iron. In the second half of the nineteenth century the Ural mines, ill served by means of communication and lacking an adequate labour supply, were rapidly surpassed by those of Russian Poland and of the Ukraine, while the eastern Ukraine (Donets Basin) became the main source of coal. At the end of the century began the large-scale exploitation of petroleum on the Baku peninsula in the Caspian (whose population were Azeri Turks, with a substantial Armenian minority).

Thus both the agricultural and the mineral wealth of the Empire came principally from the non-Russian areas. The factory industry which arose at the end of the century was, however, mainly to be found in territories of Russian population, especially in St. Petersburg, in Moscow and in central Russia. Thus the familiar pattern of metropolitan industry and colonial raw materials applied no less to the Russian than to other empires. It is of course true that Russian economic development brought material benefits to all subjects of the empire, whether Russian or not. A growing railway network, a unified system of comparatively efficient modern administration, and a single currency and customs area were great advantages. But these could of course be found in other empires too.

*　*　*

In education the Russian Empire made slow progress in the nineteenth century. The system was much better at the higher than the lower levels. Russian universities in 1900 were as good as the universities of other European countries. Primary education, however, left a great deal to be desired. Alexander I, who set up the Ministry of Education in 1802, intended, as soon as public funds and trained teachers could be made available, to give the chance of education to any of his subjects who showed ability. But under his successors

27

this policy was consciously abandoned in favour of limiting education to the upper classes. Count S. S. Uvarov, Minister of Education from 1832 to 1849, felt that education was a dangerous thing, which could put harmful ideas into the heads of humble people, and had best be confined to a select few. This policy was continued beyond the end of the century. As late as 1887 Count I. D. Delyanov, Minister of Education from 1882 to 1898, instructed his subordinates to discourage 'children of coachmen, cooks, washerwomen and people of that sort' from getting an education above their station.

Within this general reactionary framework, it was unlikely that the non-Russian peoples would do well. Alexander I had permitted the establishment of universities at Vilna and Dorpat, in which the language of instruction and the form of culture should be respectively Polish and German. After the Polish war of 1830–1831 the university of Vilna was closed, the schools of Lithuania were removed from any Polish influence, and even in the former Kingdom of Poland the instruction was increasingly Russified. The attack on the German schools in the Baltic provinces came in the late 1880's. In 1893 Dorpat university was closed, and was later reopened under another name with instruction in Russian. In the Moslem regions the situation was in some respects better. It is true that they were poor, and that the government spent little money on education. But private individuals were more easily permitted to found schools than in the non-Russian provinces in the West. The main centre was Kazan. The Tatars of the middle Volga possessed a larger proportion of rich, public-spirited and cultured men than any of the other Russian Moslems. Tatar merchants, trading under the protection of the Russian flag with Central Asia, accumulated considerable though not vast fortunes, and devoted a substantial part of their money to founding modern schools. Hitherto the Moslems had been able to go only to the traditional Koranic schools, which gave them a grounding in Moslem culture but in no way prepared them for the needs of the modern world. The new schools laid emphasis on secular learning, both humane and scientific. The most eminent pioneer was a Crimean Tatar, Ismail Bey Gaspirali (or Gasprinski), who founded a model school in Bakhche-Saray in the Crimea in 1884. It was copied especially in the Volga region. Such schools were known as 'new method' schools (*usul jadid*), and Tatar democratic reformers in general came to be known as 'Jadids'. By 1914 there were about 5000 schools of this type among Russian Moslems. The movement also had some support in Azerbaidjan and in Turkestan, and even in the protectorates of Bokhara and Khiva, though in Central Asia as a whole the backwardness of the people and the strength of narrow Islamic traditionalism were formidable barriers. In general it must be said that though the Russian government did not encourage or help the movement, and indeed did not like it, it did not seriously obstruct it.

*　　*　　*

The social policies of the Russian Empire were extremely conservative. In Russia as a whole the government supported the interests of the large landowners and of the business-men, both Russian and foreign (French, English, German and others). The peasants and workers remained poor, whether they were Russian or not. However, the interests of the Tsar and the government (as interpreted by those in power) took precedence over those of the upper classes, and where they were in conflict the people sometimes benefited. Two cases deserve mention. In Poland after the rising of 1863 a far-reaching distribution of land took place. The Russian government rightly believed that the leaders of the Polish national movement against Russia were the landowning class. It drew the conclusion that this class should be weakened, and that if the peasants were given the land they might prove more loyal subjects of the Tsar than their former landlords. Not only White Russian and Ukrainian tenants of Polish landlords in the Lithuanian borderlands, but also Polish tenants in the purely Polish provinces, received considerable amounts of land on financial terms much more favourable than had been granted to the Russian peasants who were given land in central Russia at the same time. This reform did not in fact make the Polish peasants any less patriotic as Poles, any more devoted to the Russian Tsar, but it did improve their material conditions. Similar action was taken some years later in Turkestan by General von Kaufmann, for the same reasons. It was hoped that the Russian administration would earn the gratitude of the unpolitical Uzbek and Tadjik peasants, while weakening the upper class who were potential leaders of rebellion. Von Kaufmann had served in Poland after 1863 and had doubtless taken the Polish reform as his model. In contrast to these two cases, the land reform which accompanied the liberation of serfs in Georgia in the 1860's was extremely unfavourable to the peasants and advantageous to the landlords.

Such legislation as was introduced in Imperial Russia to the advantage of industrial workers was applicable as much to non-Russians as to Russians. The working class of the Empire was predominantly Russian, but there were Azeri and Armenian workers in Baku, Georgian workers in Tiflis, Tatar workers in the Urals, German and Latvian workers in Riga, and Polish workers in the western provinces. These were drawn into the strikes and revolutionary activities of 1905–1906. In 1906 trade unions were made legal, but they had very few powers and strikes remained illegal right up to 1917.

* * *

Autocracy, centralism, preoccupation with frontier security, religious intolerance, economic exploitation and reactionary cultural and social policies were factors unfavourable to the interests of the non-Russian peoples. But it was only at the end of the nineteenth century that the government began to adopt a conscious policy of Russification. The previous policies had been made in the name of a monarch responsible to God. Russification was a policy made in the name of the Russian nation. It assumed that

Russians were superior to the other subjects of the Tsar, and that the Tsar had an obligation to prefer Russians to others. It was in a sense a democratic policy, for it appealed to the will of the nation rather than of the ruler. Not without reason had it been rejected by the absolutist Tsar Nicholas I in the first half of the century. The driving force behind Russification was the Russian bureaucracy, whose numbers and power had grown as a result of two main processes—the industrialisation of Russia and the influx into the government machine of children of the nobility for whom there was no longer room as landowners in the countryside. Industrialisation increased the complexity of the government machine and the demand for officials. The recruits from the nobility brought with them a narrowly patriotic and militarist outlook utterly different from the 'bourgeois ethos' which marked the civil services of the West European countries of this period. Russification aimed at reducing all Russian subjects to a common denominator. Even nations which had shown themselves utterly loyal to the Tsar, such as the Baltic Germans, were now pressed to adopt the Russian language, religion and way of life. The separate status of Finland was attacked. As long as their autonomy had been respected by the Tsar-Grand Duke, the Finns had been completely loyal. From 1898 onwards their liberties were whittled away, and they were turned into bitter enemies of Russia. Russification was directed with special energy against Ukrainians and Tatars, but on the whole spared both the Christian Georgians and Armenians and the Moslem peoples of Turkestan. After the revolution of 1905 all the non-Russian peoples enjoyed a period of greater freedom, but after 1907 Russification set in once more. Indeed one may say that in the last years before 1914 Russification was the unifying ideology of those political and social forces on which the new system, half-autocratic and half-constitutional, associated with the name of P. A. Stolypin, Prime Minister 1906–1911, was based. Instead of a God-ordained autocracy responsible to no man, there was a nationalist monarchy, more democratic in the sense that it was based on the mass support of Russian nationalism, directed against both non-Russians within the Empire and foreign nations. Here too there is a parallel with the mass-supported imperialism of the European states of the period 1890–1914. It is not sufficiently recognised, either by Russian or by foreign historians, that this was a genuinely popular policy, and that Russian chauvinism was no less capable of mobilising city mobs than Russian revolutionary socialism.

The occasions on which this mass chauvinism was most strikingly manifested were the *pogroms* of Jews in the towns of the Ukraine, White Russia, Lithuania, Bessarabia and Poland. The crowds of workers, artisans, peasants and lower middle class people who smashed Jewish shops and beat or killed Jews consisted not so much of Russians as of Ukrainians, Poles, White Russians, Lithuanians and Roumanians. Anti-semitism has been described as 'the socialism of the imbecile', by which is meant that anti-capitalist feeling is diverted against Jewish capitalists, and the desire for social revolution perverted into the desire to maltreat or destroy Jews. But anti-semitism in the Russian Empire was also 'the nationalism of the imbecile' in the sense that it diverted the national feeling of subject nationalities away from the dominant Russian nation and its government against the scapegoat Jews. It was certainly so understood by the Russian police authorities, who deliberately encouraged *pogroms*. A similar case was the incitation to riots in the multi-national city of Baku. Here the Armenians had some of the qualities of the Jews elsewhere, their talents as capitalists. They were a natural object of envy to the poorer and more primitive Azeri Turks, who formed the unskilled and irregularly employed urban poor of this rapidly growing city. Massacres of Armenians by Azeris and reprisals by Armenians against Azeris were a frequent feature of Trans-caucasia in the last years of the Imperial Russian regime. They were by no means unwelcome to the authorities.

*   *   *

In Imperial Russia political parties were not permitted until after 1905, and direct political criticism of government policies could not be publicly expressed. Nevertheless political ideas spread, and political groups were formed, among both Russians and non-Russians. Among the latter the national factor tended to predominate over the social, though this was not always the case. In general, however, all nationalist movements aimed also at political democracy and at considerable social reforms. Many went beyond this, and advocated some form of socialism. In most cases the national aim was self-government within the Russian Empire, rather than the creation of a separate state or incorporation in a neighbouring state.

*　　*　　*

The ultimate aim of most Poles was an independent united Poland. But as a second-best they would gladly have accepted self-government for Russian Poland within the Russian Empire, in the hope that this autonomous Poland might at some later stage, with Russian help, acquire also those parts of Poland which belonged to the German and Austrian empires. However, a restoration of the Kingdom of 1815 would not have satisfied them. They required a more democratic system of government, and they wished Poland to include at least a large part of the Lithuanian borderlands, if possible to stretch as far east as the frontier of 1772, before the First Partition. There was also a school of thought which regarded Russia as the main enemy of Poland, and preferred to go with Austria, and even with Germany, against Russia. A third point of view was that of the left wing of the Polish socialist movement, which considered national independence less important than social revolution. The extreme left leader, Roza Luxemburg, even stated that Polish independence was positively undesirable, and that it was the best interest of the Polish working class to remain permanently divided between the three great empires, and great economic units, of Russia, Austria-Hungary and Germany.

*　　*　　*

Ukrainian nationalist parties, which grew quickly from the beginning of the century, mostly stood for some form of socialism. They hoped for autonomy for the Ukraine within a democratic Russia, and hoped that Austrian-ruled Eastern Galicia would be added to them. In Galicia, however, the Ukrainian nationalists were more uncompromising. Their aim was a completely independent Ukrainian state. They hoped to achieve this with Austrian and German help. They reckoned that the gain to Austria from the consequent dismemberment of the Russian Empire might induce the Austrian government to agree to part with Eastern Galicia. This extreme nationalist point of view had little support within the Russian Ukraine.

In Bessarabia there was little political activity among the Roumanians. But such as had political aims would have preferred union with the existing independent state of Roumania, that is to say, the restoration of the unity of historical Moldavia, which had been broken by the Russian annexation of 1812.

*　　*　　*

In the Baltic provinces, the second half of the nineteenth century had brought an awakening of national feeling among the educated class of the Estonian and Latvian peoples. In this the most active elements had been Protestant pastors and school teachers. It was at first mainly anti-German, since the Germans formed the upper social class and controlled the power and wealth. Estonians and Latvians even regarded Russia to some extent as a protector against German domination. This attitude changed with the Russification policy of the 1890's. In 1905 there were bloody strikes and peasant revolts in Latvia. Marxist socialism was strong in Latvia, especially in Riga, but not in Estonia. At this time national independence was not considered a practical, or perhaps even a desirable, aim in either country. The Germans of the Baltic on the whole remained loyal to Russia, but with decreasing conviction as Russification continued. The younger generation to some extent hoped for salvation from a successful war by the German Empire against Russia.

In Transcaucasia by far the strongest political group in Georgia was moderate Marxist socialism (Menshevism). The Georgian Mensheviks were definitely against national independence, and were not even interested in national self-government. Their aim was an all-Russian democratic republic. The strongest Armenian group, the *Dashnaktsutiun* (Revolutionary Federation), was both nationalist and socialist. But its national aim was the liberation of Armenia from the Turks, for which it needed the help of Russia. A greater Armenian homeland within the Russian Empire would have been acceptable. The Azeri Turks were affected by the democratic modernising movement among the Moslems of the Empire. They did not especially wish to be separated from Russia. They shared their language with the Turks of the Ottoman Empire (with which their country did not have a common border), and their religion (the Shia branch of Islam) with the Persians. Neither the Ottoman Empire nor the Persia of the Kadjar dynasty made much appeal to modern-educated and politically minded Azeris. The various peoples of the Caucasus range were hardly touched by political ideas. They were not nationalists but Moslems. Hostility to Russia, still powerful in a latent form, was on religious rather than national grounds.

*   *   *

The most politically active Moslems in Russia were the Tatars of the Volga valley. They had both business-men and a modern-educated intellectual elite, among whom school teachers were especially important. The most widespread political attitude among them was a radical liberalism, but a minority were socialists. All stood for democratic liberties, education for all, and emancipation of women. They did not hope to create an independent Tatar state. They realised that the existence of the Russian Empire was in a sense to their advantage, for within it they formed an elite among all Moslems. Their influence was felt even in the Kazakh steppes and Turkestan, as well as in Crimea and Azerbaidjan. They did not even wish for territorial autonomy, for the Tatars were too scattered to lay claim to any compact homeland of their own. Rather they wished to secure the full respect of the state for the rights of Moslems, as equal citizens speaking their own language, in whatever part of the Empire they might live.

But there was a trend of thought, which to some extent affected most politically conscious Tatars, and which potentially conflicted with their loyalty to the Russian Empire. This was Pan-Turkism, the idea of a common culture and a common nationality among all whose native tongue was one of the Turkic language group (Ottoman Turkish, Azeri, Tatar, Kazakh, Turkmen, Uzbek). Indeed one may say that the Volga Tatars developed the idea of a Turkish nation, whose distinctive mark was the Turkish language, at a time when this idea was still unknown among the Turks of the Ottoman Empire, who had not yet distinguished Turkish nationality either from the religious community of Islam or from the political category of Ottoman citizenship. In this sense the Volga Tatar nationalists were the spiritual ancestors of the Turkish nationalism of Kemal Atatürk. The Tatar intellectuals tried to develop a single Turkish language, based on Ottoman Turkish, for all Turkic peoples of the Russian Empire. The pioneer of this idea was Gasprinski, the founder of the *jadid* school of Bakhche-Saray, who also founded a bilingual newspaper, in Russian and Turkish, entitled *Terjumen* (The Interpreter), which was widely read even as far as Turkestan. But the attempt to reduce the Turkic languages of the Volga, the Crimea, Transcaucasia and Central Asia to a common tongue was a failure.

When the first Russian parliament, the Duma, was created in 1906, there were Moslem members. Their numbers were greatly reduced when the franchise was narrowed in 1907, but a remnant was left. These Moslem leaders for a time hoped that Russia and Ottoman Turkey would co-operate with each other, that there would be a friendship between the two states which had large Turkic populations, and that the Russian Tatars could play a mediating role. But it soon became clear that Russian policy was opposed to that of Turkey, and that Russia would back the Balkan Christian enemies of the Sultan. Some of the Tatar leaders emigrated to Turkey, and supported the cause of the Central Powers in the First World War. Others relapsed into passivity.

* * *

In Central Asia the *jadid* movement had a small following. On the other hand, hostility to Russia based on traditional memories and on religious conviction remained strong. Neither of these forces was politically effective. The main new source of conflict in these years between Russians and Central Asians was the growing colonisation of Russian peasants in the Kazakh steppes, and to a lesser extent in Turkestan. A further cause of resentment came in the third year of the First World War. In June 1916 the Russian government called up the people of Central Asia for labour service in the rear of the war fronts. This, added to other existing causes of discontent, provided the occasion for a series of bloody risings, ruthlessly repressed, in various parts of Turkestan, Turkmenia and the Kazakh steppes.

The multi-national Russian Empire, 55% of whose subjects were not Russians, entered the First World War in August 1914 with its social and national conflicts far from solution. Defeat in the war brought revolution, and revolution offered new opportunities to the subject peoples. When the Bolsheviks led by Lenin seized power in the second revolution, of November 1917, the 'national problem' was one of the most important that confronted them.

3

The Bolshevik Revolution

LENIN believed, as a Marxist should, that nationality, like religion, was a product of a certain stage in the development of human society, and would disappear in more advanced stages. Nationalism, the political doctrine that the boundaries of states should be based on the nationality of their inhabitants, and that any nation which desired it should have the right to self-government, or even to an independent state of its own, was clearly connected with the growth of capitalism and the formation of bourgeois classes. When the capitalist system gave way to socialism, nationalism would gradually lose its power and disappear. Nationalism was not one of the basic factors in human history: these were economic. The driving force of human history was provided by the changes in productive forces and productive relations, from which came the class struggle.

Nevertheless, in the short term, nationalism was a powerful political force, and Lenin was far too great a realist not to recognise it. Within the Russian Empire there was a growing nationalism directed against the dominant Great Russians, and in many cases there were also national conflicts between different subject nations. In so far as these conflicts could be manipulated by the Russian government (for example, the conflict between Armenians and Azeri Turks), they diverted discontent from its natural economic and social objectives and so damaged the revolutionary cause. But in so far as they could be manipulated by revolutionaries, they could become a valuable additional force of hostility to the government, and could benefit the revolutionary cause.

Lenin sincerely rejected the domination of one nation

over another, just as he rejected the exploitation of the workers and peasants by the landowners and bourgeoisie. There was clearly no room for nationalist oppression or discrimination within a socialist state of the future. On this all socialists were nominally agreed. But various possible solutions to the problem could be suggested. One was advanced by the Austrian socialists Otto Bauer and Karl Renner. It was that every citizen should have a personal nationality which should be respected by the government, and in matters of national culture should be governed by an autonomous institution elected by members of the same nationality, regardless of where they lived. This cultural autonomy should be combined with political centralism: on all matters not affecting individual national cultures, the central government's authority should be equally binding on all its subjects. This scheme was specially devised for the circumstances of the multi-national Austro-Hungarian Monarchy, in which, apart from certain major areas of compact population, there were many smaller communities scattered over wide areas. In the Russian Empire too these conditions were to be found. For example, there were German, Polish, Jewish, Tatar and Armenian communities of varying size in many parts of European Russia, the Caucasus and Central Asia. Another type of solution for the problem of nationality was of course federalism. Each major region of compact nationality was to be self-governing, and the regions were to be united only for purposes of common interest to all, such as foreign policy, defence and currency. The outstanding model of federal government was of course the United States, but various forms of semi-federal or confederal government could be found in the history of nineteenth-century Germany.

*   *   *

Lenin rejected both federal government and the Bauer scheme of national cultural autonomy. He believed that socialist states should be centralised and homogeneous. At the same time he believed that any nation which wished to set up its own centralised state should be free to do so. The same principle applied to the socialist party, as Lenin conceived it. Within the party there could be no special autonomy for party members of a particular nationality or religion (as, for example, the Jewish socialist organisation in Russia, the *Bund*, claimed). In Lenin's view, a separate working class should be entitled to its own socialist party, but anyone who became a member of his Bolshevik party must unconditionally accept its orders in all matters, and claim no special status because he belonged to some nation other than Russian. Lenin therefore stood on the one hand for absolute centralism in his own Bolshevik (later renamed Communist) Party, and on the other hand for the right of self-determination of every nationality within the Russian Empire. At the same time he hoped that the nationalities would choose not to be separated. They should have the right of self-determination, but they should also have the right of fusion. Lenin certainly had no preference for a multiplicity of small states. He did, however, insist that it was for them to decide, and that it was impermissible that the dominant nation (in the Russian case the Great Russians) should decide on their behalf.

However, the application in practice of the doctrine of 'self-determination up to the point of secession' was not easy. The nationalities were not politically united. To which political group was the right to decide to belong? Should the strongest political group be accepted as representing the will of the nation, even if it was led by conservatives or by bourgeois liberals, and was fighting against those of its compatriots who were socialists? Or should a socialist group be recognised as representative, and receive military aid from the Bolsheviks, even if it was supported only by a minority of its compatriots? In the theoretical discussions of the 'national question' by the Bolsheviks before the Revolution, no clear answer was found to this question.

*   *   *

When Lenin seized power in November 1917, the Russian

Empire was already threatened with dissolution by national movements among the non-Russians, which had made considerable headway since the first revolution in March. The most important areas to be briefly considered are the western borderlands, the Ukraine, Transcaucasia and Tatar lands.

The collapse of Tsardom gave the Finns the chance to break away from Russia. Their experience of Russification in the last twenty years had convinced them that nothing less than complete independence was possible. In the Baltic provinces the German element, impressed by the victories of the German armies and remembering the similar Russification policies, which had been only partly modified after 1906, was hoping for union with Germany, while the Estonians and Latvians were now about equally hostile to Germans and Russians. The areas of compact Polish population were at this time under German military occupation, and the Germans were advancing into the Lithuanian borderlands.

In the Ukraine a group of radical intellectuals had set up, soon after the March revolution, a Ukrainian national council (*Rada*). This was at first chiefly concerned with cultural matters, with ensuring complete freedom to use the Ukrainian language in speech and print. During the next months it became a much more representative body, supported by the main political parties of the Ukraine and by organisations of soldiers, peasants and workers, and turned itself into a provisional parliament of the Ukraine, with its own provisional executive body, the General Secretariat. It conducted negotiations with the Provisional Government in Petrograd but failed to reach real agreement. At the time of the Bolshevik Revolution, the *Rada* was the nearest approach to an effective authority in the Ukraine, and stood for far-reaching autonomy for the Ukraine within some sort of federal Russian republic.

In Transcaucasia neither the Armenians nor the Georgians wished to separate from Russia, while the Azeri Turks were involved in the political argument which now broke out among the politically minded elements of all the main Moslem groups in Russia.

On 14 May 1917 there met in Moscow an All-Russian Moslem Congress, with representatives sent by the main regions of Moslem population. Two main points of view were expressed. The representatives of the borderlands, Azerbaidjan and Central Asia in particular, wished for territorial self-government within Russia. The Volga Tatars, who lacked a compact territory but had communities scattered over Russia, put forward a plan for combining cultural autonomy for all Moslems with a centralised government for the Russian republic, which closely resembled the ideas of the Austrian socialists Bauer and Renner. The border peoples opposed this not only because they were primarily interested in the needs of their own regions but also because they had a certain distrust of the Tatars, the best educated and socially most developed of the Russian Moslems. They believed, not without reason, that if the central institution for handling Moslem cultural affairs, proposed by the Tatars, had been created, it would have been dominated by Tatars although nominally representing all Moslems, and would have led to a kind of 'Tatarisation' of Central Asia. The policy of territorial self-government therefore won a substantial majority at the Congress. The Congress set up a Moslem National Council (*Shura*) to bring Moslem views to the notice of the Russian government.

* * *

When he had seized power in November 1917, Lenin was resolved to deal with this fluid situation among the non-Russian peoples by putting his policy of 'self-determination' into practice. But everything depended on the terms on which peace could be concluded with Germany and her allies. The Bolshevik government was in fact forced to accept, by the Treaty of Brest-Litovsk of March 1918 and certain other decisions which resulted from it, the loss of all the western borderlands, the Ukraine and Transcaucasia. These must be briefly considered in turn.

The Bolsheviks recognised the independence of Finland. But at the end of January 1918 civil war broke out between the socialists and the conservative nationalists. Some Russian troops stationed in Finland, who were loyal to the Bolsheviks, gave some assistance to the Finnish socialist forces, while the Finnish conservatives enlisted some military support from the Germans. The fighting was however mainly between Finns, and ended in May 1918 in the victory of the Right. The Baltic provinces were occupied by the German army, and the local German element ruled under protection of William II's generals. Poland was also under German rule. In the White Russian borderlands there was a struggle at the end of 1917 between White Russian nationalists and a White Russian Bolshevik authority based on Minsk. The advancing German army set up a puppet White Russian administration of its own. In Lithuania too there was a regime protected by the Germans, which proclaimed the independence of a Lithuanian state in February 1918. In Bessarabia at the end of 1917 a Council of the Land (*Sfatul Tserii*) was set up which represented the most politically conscious elements of the Roumanian population. In January 1918 it appealed to the government of Roumania to send troops to protect it against the local forces loyal to the Bolsheviks. On 9 April 1918 the Council voted for the union of Bessarabia with Roumania.

Though the Bolsheviks recognised the right of the Ukrainian people to self-determination, they had no intention of allowing the *Rada* to exercise the right. They hoped to raise organised support for their regime in the Ukraine, relying especially on the workers of the large cities, a large part of whom were not Ukrainian but Russian. An all-Ukrainian Congress of workers' soviets was held in Kiev in December 1917, but only a minority of its members were Bolsheviks. This minority then walked out of the congress and proceeded to the second city of the Ukraine, Kharkov, where they organised their own counter-congress, and set up in its name a rival Ukrainian government. In nominal support of this Kharkov government, Bolshevik troops in

January 1918 invaded the Ukraine. The *Rada* leaders appealed to the Germans, who recognised the independence of the Ukraine, occupied its territory and forced the Bolsheviks to recognise it by the Treaty of Brest-Litovsk. Thus Russia lost its most valuable grain lands and its most developed metallurgical industry.

In Transcaucasia the main political parties—the Georgian Mensheviks, Armenian *Dashnaktsutiun* and the democratic party of the Azeri Tatars, *Musavat* (Equality)—set up a local provisional government, the Transcaucasian Commissariat. Their final breach with the Bolsheviks was caused by their rejection of those parts of the Treaty of Brest-Litovsk which ceded territory in Transcaucasia to Germany's ally, Turkey. On 22 April they proclaimed an independent Transcaucasian Federal Republic. A month later, the disagreements between the three constituent nations led to its disintegration into three separate republics of Georgia, Armenia and Azerbaidjan. Georgia placed itself under the protection of the Germans, who guaranteed it against further Turkish claims. Armenia was rapidly overrun by the Turks. In Azerbaidjan, the industrial city of Baku was held by Russian and Armenian political groups (first Bolsheviks, then moderate socialists), while the *Musavat* controlled the countryside and co-operated with the advancing Turkish army. In September 1918 Baku fell to the Turks.

Thus during 1918 Lenin's government had no authority over the Ukraine, Transcaucasia or the western borderlands, but was more or less effective in northern and central Russia, and until the summer in most of Russia in Asia. Within this large, though reduced, area the 'national question' for the Bolsheviks consisted in practice of the relationship with the Moslem peoples—with the Tatars and with Central Asia.

* * *

The most accessible of the Moslems to Bolshevik influence were the Volga Tatars, who had a considerable intellectual elite, a minority of which were socialists. Lenin's chief adviser on the problems of the non-Russian peoples was J. V. Stalin, who was appointed People's Commissar of Nationalities in the Bolshevik government. In January 1918 was established a Central Moslem Commissariat for the Interior of Russia, whose chairman was a Tatar named Mulla Nur Vakhitov. Meanwhile the *Shura*, set up by the Moslem congress of May 1917, still existed in Petrograd, and had subordinate provincial organs of its own, the two most important being in Kazan and Ufa. In Kazan was also sitting a Moslem Assembly (*Medzhlis*). In February 1918 the *Medzhlis* proclaimed itself in favour of a Volga-Ural autonomous state, and ordered preparations for the creation of a constituent assembly for the people of this region. This the Bolsheviks prevented by force. Their troops in Kazan, consisting of Russian soldiers and reinforced by Russian units sent from Moscow, captured the Tatar quarter of the city after serious fighting, and suppressed the *Medzhlis* and other provincial organisations of the Moslem movement.

Vakhitov was able to recruit a certain number of Tatars, and to form Tatar military units, in support of the Bolshevik government, which acted through Vakhitov's Commissariat. In March a Tatar-Bashkir soviet republic of the Russian Soviet Federation was proclaimed. It was the Bolsheviks' alternative to the Volga-Ural state proposed by the defeated Moslem nationalists. It was to be ruled by local communists. Its area was so devised as to include large areas inhabited by Russians, and also by smaller national groups, the Chuvash and Cheremiss: the Tatars and Bashkirs were not an absolute majority of its population. In June 1918 Vakhitov called a conference of provincial branches of his Commissariat, and founded a Russian Party of Moslem Communists, with its own Central Committee. Shortly afterwards, however, large-scale civil war in Russia started with the armed clash between the Czech legions and the Bolshevik forces, and with the formation of an anti-Bolshevik administration under Czech protection. The Czechs took Kazan, and among their prisoners was Vakhitov, who was executed. For the next year the Volga-Ural area was the scene of civil war between the Russian Red and White armies. The lands of the Tatars were ravaged by each side in turn, and plans for their future had to be postponed.

In the southern Urals the Bashkirs, closely related to the Tatars but far less influenced by modern ideas, found a leader in Zeki Validov, who was arrested by the Bolsheviks in Orenburg in February 1918, but escaped and organised a small Bashkir armed force with which he fought on the White side. But the uncompromising Russian imperialism of Admiral Kolchak and the officers of the White armies caused him to break with the Whites and make an agreement with the Bolsheviks. In return for the promise of an Autonomous Bashkir Republic, to be ruled by an elected revolutionary committee (*Bashrevkom*), Validov brought his forces over to the Red side in February 1919.

In the Kazakh steppes a nationalist group had appeared in 1917 called *Alash-Orda*, led essentially by the modern-educated intellectual elite. Its leaders in 1918 co-operated with the Whites, but like the Bashkirs they were antagonised by the unbending Russian imperialism of Kolchak. In the summer of 1919, when it was clear that the Whites were losing in Siberia, and when the Bolsheviks were promising freedom to the nationalities and amnesties to their former opponents, many Kazakhs, including the prominent nationalist leader Akhmed Baitursunov, went over to the Red side.

In Turkestan the capital city of Tashkent, which had a large Russian population of railway workers and officials, was taken over by Bolsheviks at the time of the November Revolution of 1917. But the countryside, with its overwhelmingly Moslem population of Uzbeks and Tadjiks, followed the Moslem nationalist leaders. The nationalists negotiated with the Bolsheviks in Tashkent. The latter however not only rejected any effective self-government for the Turkestan Moslems, but even objected to the inclusion of Moslems in the Bolshevik administration of the region. The Russian workers and small officials of Tashkent in fact showed themselves more narrowly chauvinist and imperialist in their attitude to the 'natives' than had the governors and officers of the Imperial Russian regime. In this respect they may be compared to the 'poor whites' of South Africa or the southern states of the United States, or to the *petits blancs* of Algeria or Senegal.

The Moslem nationalists held a congress in Kokand at the end of November 1917, and elected a provisional assembly and a provisional government. In February 1918 however the Tashkent Bolsheviks captured Kokand and massacred most of the city's population. In March they invaded the protectorate of Bokhara, but were defeated. The greater part of Turkestan nevertheless remained under Tashkent's authority. The Moslems were subjected to a reign of terror. A communist authority in 1921 described the regime as 'feudal exploitation of the broad masses of the native population by the Russian Red-Army-man, colonist and official'. The government in Moscow received some information of what was going on, and sent repeated protests and directives, but these had virtually no effect. It was not until the end of 1919, when the White armies in Siberia had been finally defeated, that the Bolshevik central government had direct physical access to Turkestan and was able to send a special commission to carry out a drastic reorganisation.

*   *   *

The collapse of Germany in November 1918 meant the end of the Brest-Litovsk settlement and the possibility of Bolshevik action in the western borderlands and in the Ukraine. Lenin quickly showed that he intended to interpret the principle of self-determination in the manner best suited to himself. Wherever possible, 'proletarian' parties were to be recognised as representing their compatriots, and therefore entitled to exercise on their behalf the choice between 'secession' and 'fusion', and it was to be the Moscow government which would decide which parties were 'proletarian'. This meant of course in practice that Red Army support would be given wherever possible to any communist party. The result of the struggle was in each case decided not by the will of the peoples but by military force.

In the Baltic states the Bolsheviks quickly intervened. An Estonian Soviet government was proclaimed in Narva, near the Russian border. It had no substantial support, and was defeated by the Estonian nationalists who took over power from the Germans. In Latvia the local communist movement, based on the working class of Riga, had genuine strength. A three-cornered struggle developed between Latvian nationalists, Latvian communists and the local German community backed by remnants of the German army. The communists held out in Riga from January to June 1919. In the end the Latvian nationalists triumphed, and Latvia like Estonia became an independent state. The same result was achieved in Lithuania, where the support for communism was negligible except in the city of Vilna, which was held by the Bolsheviks for a short time early in 1919 but was then captured by the Polish army. In White Russia the Bolsheviks established a government in Minsk, but to the west there was a no-man's-land of intermittent fighting between it and the resurgent Polish state.

In the Ukraine the defeat of Germany led to a struggle between the Bolsheviks and the left-wing Ukrainian nationalists. In February 1919 the Red Army occupied the greater part of the Ukraine. During 1919 a new force appeared in the Russian White Army of General Denikin. Supplied with arms and equipment by the Western Powers, Denikin swept through the Ukraine and arrived within 250 miles of Moscow. Denikin was, however, defeated by the Red Army, and rapidly retreated south.

The Ukraine, however, became the scene of one more military campaign in April 1920, when the Polish army invaded it. The Poles captured Kiev, but their success soon turned to failure. The Ukrainian population gave them no help. The Polish army retreated, and the retreat turned into a rout. The Red Army pursued them, and in the Polish city of Bialystok set up a provisional puppet government of Polish communists, led by the Polish-born head of the Bolshevik security police, Feliks Dzherzhinski. Pilsudski counter-attacked, and the Red Army retreated into Russia. An armistice was signed, and peace negotiations ended in the Treaty of Riga of March 1921. White Russia and Ukraine were partitioned between Poland and Russia. During 1920 the Bolshevik government also signed treaties of peace with Estonia, Latvia and Lithuania, establishing with these three countries frontiers which corresponded fairly closely to the ethnic boundaries.

* * *

The Transcaucasian republics survived the defeat of the Central Powers, and the Western Powers gave them *de facto* recognition. The Armenians indeed hoped greatly to extend their country's frontiers, to include large parts of eastern Asia Minor and even to reach the north-east corner of the Mediterranean. Azerbaidjan was basically a weak state because its capital was inhabited, and its petroleum industry worked, by Russian and Armenian workers who preferred Soviet Russia to independent Azerbaidjan. By far the healthiest of the three was Georgia, whose Menshevik government enjoyed great popular support, and set to work to establish a small social democratic republic which won the admiration of those Europeans who visited it in the next two years.

But none of the three republics survived. This was partly because they quarrelled with each other, and because they failed sufficiently to interest Western opinion in their cause. But the decisive factor was the success of the Turkish Revolution. When Kemal Atatürk defied the European victors, his only friend was Soviet Russia. Independent Transcaucasian states could not exist except when Russia and Turkey were hostile to each other, and the one wished to use a small client state against the other. But now Russia and Turkey were associated in hostility to the West. The Turks were determined to retain their Armenian provinces, and Russia had no interest in preventing them. The Bolsheviks were determined to get their hands on Baku's oil and to help the Baku proletariat, and Kemal Atatürk was not interested in saving the Azeri Turks from Russian rule.

In April 1920 the Red Army invaded Azerbaidjan, its action being synchronised with a rising by Bolsheviks in Baku. In November 1920 the rump republic of Armenia, the territory which had formerly belonged to the Russian Empire, was likewise occupied. It seemed just possible that Georgia might survive. In May 1920 the Bolshevik government even signed a treaty with it. However, this did not save the small republic. In February 1921 the Red Army invaded. This action was above all the work of Stalin, who had old personal rancours against the Georgian Mensheviks. Lenin was unhappy about it, and urged a conciliatory policy. In practice, however, opposition was ruthlessly crushed.

The chaos of 1917–1920 provided opportunities for the small mountain peoples of the Caucasus, who had never accepted in their hearts their conquest by Russia, to seek their freedom. But they were too small, too heterogeneous and too backward to have any hope of success. They fought at various times against both Russian Whites and Russian Reds, and were cruelly treated by both. At the end of 1920 Bolshevik authority was more or less reasserted. Communist party members were in control, but the outward appearance of self-government was provided by the creation in January 1921 of the Daghestan Autonomous Soviet Socialist Republic and by the Mountaineers' ASSR (composed of the peoples of the Terek region).

*　　*　　*

The defeat of the Whites made possible a more permanent organisation of the Tatar and Bashkir lands. Already in November 1918 the separate Russian Party of Moslem Communists was dissolved: in its place was a Central Bureau of Moslem Organisations of the Russian Communist Party, placed directly under the Central Committee of the RCP. It was decided to abandon the idea of a Tatar-Bashkir republic, and to form a separate Tatar ASSR. This was created in September 1920. In Bashkiria the *Bashrevkom* led by Validov soon came into conflict with the Bolshevik leaders, who interpreted in their own sense, of complete subjection to the Russian Communist Party, the promises of autonomy that they had made in 1919. In the summer of 1920 there was a national Bashkir rising against the Russians, and the Red Army suppressed it by force and occupied the country. The Bashkir ASSR which was set up at the end of 1920 was controlled by Russian communists. During 1920 and 1921 separate autonomous republics or autonomous regions were also set up for the smaller peoples of the Volga valley, the Chuvash, Mari and Votyaks. Thus nothing remained of the dream of a Tatar-dominated Volga-Ural state.

In Turkestan widespread Moslem resistance to the Tashkent authorities continued in the form of a guerrilla movement known as the *Basmachi*. This was not suppressed until the end of 1922, and some resistance continued even longer. The Bolsheviks also in 1920 invaded the protectorates of Khiva and Bokhara, the second of which had successfully resisted an attack from Tashkent in 1918. The conquered territories were converted into the Soviet People's Republics of Khorezm and Bokhara. The purpose of this new title was to show that the government was not 'socialist' because it was not in the hands of a socialist party. Government was nominally shared by left-wing modernist Moslems (*Jadidists*) and communists. The Soviet government signed treaties with both republics, recognising their sovereignty and claiming only certain economic privileges for Soviet Russia. In practice however the pressure of Moscow through the local communists increased, and in 1924 both republics were abolished and their territory subdivided among the new republics of Soviet Central Asia.

*　　*　　*

The Soviet government continued the policy of Imperial Russia in maintaining a predominant influence in Mongolia, but went considerably further. Mongolia was in fact converted into a communist-ruled satellite of the Soviet Union.

In 1919 the Soviet government announced that it repudiated the privileges formerly enjoyed in Mongolia by the Imperial Russian government. In October 1919 the Chinese government sent General Hsu Shu-tseng to restore Chinese authority in Mongolia. In February 1921 a former Imperial Russian officer, Baron Ungern-Sternberg, who had a private army of his own, composed partly of Russians and partly of Tunguses and partly financed and officered by Japanese, entered Mongolia, and was for a time welcomed as a deliverer from Chinese rule. Meanwhile some left-wing Mongolian revolutionaries, led by Sukhe Bator and Choibalsan, had taken refuge in the territory of the Far Eastern Republic, the fictional buffer state maintained under Bolshevik control, with its capital at Irkutsk, from the beginning of 1920 till the end of 1922. The Mongol exiles held a conference in March 1921 at Kyakhta, near the border with Mongolia, founded a Mongolian Revolutionary People's Party, formed a 'people's government', and appealed for the aid of the Red Army. In May Ungern-Sternberg attacked Soviet territory, but was defeated, captured and shot. The Red Army advanced into Mongolia, entered its capital of Urga on 6 July, and set up a government with the lama Bodo as Prime Minister and Sukhe Bator as Minister of War. In November 1921 a treaty of alliance was signed between Soviet Russia and the Mongolian People's Republic. An area to the west of Mongolia was in 1922 made into a People's Republic of Tannu Tuva, which became a protectorate of Soviet Russia though not as yet incorporated in it.

To most Mongols the traditional enemies were the Chinese, and the attitude to Russia was on the whole friendly. Thus at first the new regime was accepted not only by the tiny left-wing revolutionary intelligentsia but also by the more conservative forces. But the Soviet communists were not prepared to leave things as they were in this traditionalist and theocratic state, ruled by Buddhist lamas.

Early in 1921 they began to introduce a programme of land redistribution, nationalisation of forests and mines and educational reform directed against Buddhist influence, and did their best to incite the population to civil war against the nobility and the lamas. In April 1922 Prime Minister Bodo and other leading Mongol politicians were arrested, accused of conspiring with China and executed. His successor, Danzan, who also became commander-in-chief of the army on the death of Sukhe Bator in 1923, was a revolutionary but also a Mongol patriot, who wished his country to remain independent, and hoped to include in a united Mongolia those regions which still remained in Russia or China. He was overthrown and executed in May 1924. During the next four years Soviet Russian influence was overwhelmingly strong, but Mongolia was still allowed to have some direct economic and cultural contact with foreign countries. The Buddhist monasteries also preserved their property and their own organisation.

Thus by the early 1920's the frontiers of the Soviet state had been fixed. Territory had been lost in the West, but there had been an expansion of control in the Far East. The decisive factors had been neither theoretical doctrine nor 'the will of the masses', but international power. The Baltic States and Finland survived because Britain could dominate the Baltic Sea. Poland and Roumania acquired territories with Ukrainian and White Russian subjects because both were backed by the military power of France. The Transcaucasian states collapsed because they had in their rear an indifferent or hostile Turkey. Wherever foreign might could not reach, the Bolsheviks reasserted the might of Russia, speaking in the name not of the Tsar but of the proletariat. The Russian Empire remained, but it was ruled on quite different principles, radically changing the lives of Russians and non-Russians alike.

4

The Soviet Empire

During the half-century which has elapsed since the communist victory in the civil war, the treatment by the Soviet government of the non-Russian nations, which have formed a little less than half the population of the Soviet Union, has varied. The variations have corresponded with the main general phases of Soviet government policy as a whole. During the years of the New Economic Policy (NEP) from 1921 to 1928 the 'nationalities' (as the non-Russian peoples are usually called in Soviet terminology) benefited from the general relaxation of pressure which made life more tolerable for all Soviet citizens. During the years of collectivisation of agriculture and the First Five Year Plan, from 1928 to 1933, the nationalities suffered terrible hardships, as did the Russians. After two years of milder conditions, the Great Purge of 1936 to 1938 hit the nationalities with special severity. In 1939 and 1940 the Soviet Union forcibly annexed large territories in Europe, bringing about twenty million more people under communist rule. The hardships of the war, from 1941 to 1945, and of the post-war reconstruction and Stalin's last years, from 1945 to 1952, had certain specific repercussions on the nationalities. Finally they, like their Russian fellow-citizens, have substantially improved their lot in the years since the death of Stalin. We must now briefly examine these different phases from the point of view of the nationalities, before analysing the main aspects of Soviet imperial rule.

The essence of the NEP period was that, while there was no compromise on the principle of absolute political power for the Communist Party, there were far-reaching cultural and economic concessions. In the non-Russian areas as in

54

Russia proper, the autocratic decisions of the Moscow government were transmitted downwards through the lower levels of the highly centralised party machine. Local soviets (the nominally representative organs of local government), trade unions, co-operatives, factory managements, the youth movement and other 'public organisations' were controlled by the party machine through the party members who held office in them.

But within this rigid framework of political power, the non-Russians did enjoy cultural advantages which they had not had under the Imperial regime. Official doctrine at this time distinguished between two 'deviations', each equally harmful, which communists must avoid. One was 'Great Russian Great-Power chauvinism', the other was 'local bourgeois nationalism'. The duty of communists of all nations of the Soviet Union was to fight against 'their own bourgeoisie'. Russian communists must insist on the right of non-Russians to full equality with Russians, in particular on the right to use their own language in public and in private, orally and in print, and to obtain responsible jobs in the administration of their region. Communists of the nationalities must insist on the duty of solidarity with the Russian people, must oppose any idea of separation from Russia and must prevent discrimination against Russian minorities living in their midst.

The Russians were, with the possible exception of the Georgians and Armenians, the best-educated and economically most advanced of the nations of the Soviet Union. It was thus inevitable that Russians should predominate in the machinery of government and in the party machine. Thus there was in practice a greater likelihood that the 'Great Russian chauvinist deviation' would make itself felt. The government in Moscow therefore in the 1920's devoted more effort to opposing it than to attacking local nationalism. It does not however follow that its efforts were always effective. There was some difference in its application in different areas.

It was in the Ukraine that this policy was most effective.

The combined efforts of Ukrainian communists and of the Moscow leaders ensured that the Ukrainians were freed from the Russification of Imperial times. The Ukrainian language was used in the conduct of public business, and as a medium of instruction in the schools. Ukrainian literature and learned publications flourished. The workers in Ukrainian industry were increasingly Ukrainian, and the cities of the Ukraine, previously strongholds of Russian influence, became 'Ukrainianised'. To the majority of the Ukrainian people, these gains probably compensated for the loss of political liberty.

The Tatars of the Volga also had perhaps gained more than they had lost. Their hopes of a Volga-Ural state had been defeated. But in the Tatar ASSR the local Tatar communists were on the whole backed by Moscow in their quarrels with the Russian communists of the region. The Tatar language was used more extensively in public business and in the schools than had been the case since the Russian conquest of Kazan in 1552. The outstanding Tatar leader was Mirza Sultan-Galiev, who in 1918 had succeeded the executed Vakhitov as Stalin's chief adviser on Moslem affairs in the Commissariat of Nationalities. Though a revolutionary communist, Sultan-Galiev had original ideas. He had retained, from the days when he was a member of the *jadid* movement, a belief in the solidarity of the Turkic peoples, including Kazakhs and Uzbeks as well as Tatars and Bashkirs and Azeris. He also had a wider conception of anti-colonial revolution in Asia. He believed that the emphasis placed by the Bolshevik leaders on revolution in industrial Europe was mistaken, and that they should devote their main attention to Asia, especially to the Moslem lands of Turkey, Persia, Afghanistan and India. His disciples were strong in Kazan and the Tatar provinces. They were as much Tatar patriots as they were communists: in practice they felt more community with Tatar peasants or small business-men (who were permitted to operate under NEP) as fellow-Tatars, than with Russian workers as fellow-proletarians.

This period of Tatar 'national communism' came to an end in 1923, when it was discovered that Sultan-Galiev had been in secret correspondence with non-communist Crimean Tatar, Bashkir and Central Asian political leaders in exile. He was dismissed from his post, and within the Tatar ASSR the Russian communists gained greater influence. Nevertheless Tatar cultural nationalism remained a considerable force.

In Transcaucasia the situation was less satisfactory. It is true that the Georgian, Armenian and Azeri languages were given official status. In Azerbaidjan, however, the Russian minority, dominating the working class and the communist party, were clearly the rulers of the country, while the Georgians and Armenians, being politically minded and sophisticated nations, bitterly resented the imposition of an alien form of government, even if it was administered by compatriots. The Soviet occupation of Armenia was followed by a massive armed revolt in 1921, which was savagely repressed. In Georgia, even the minority of Georgian Bolsheviks soon came into conflict with the policies of their compatriot from Moscow, Joseph Stalin, and many of their leaders were dismissed from their newly acquired posts. In August 1924 there was a large-scale peasant rising in Georgia against the regime, and this too was savagely repressed.

*　　*　　*

In Central Asia the attempts of the Moscow government to break the grip of Russian 'poor white' chauvinists in the party apparatus, though sincerely pursued, were only partly successful. It was extremely difficult to find Asians who were not only sufficiently educated to perform skilled jobs in administration or economic management but at the same time were free from the 'bourgeois nationalist' desire to free their country from Russian rule. Therefore Russians continued to play a leading part. The foundations were, however, laid of a system of education in vernacular languages which would ultimately produce an Asian educated elite. Meanwhile the social reforms which were carried out were not necessarily either popular or beneficial to the natives. The emancipation of women, desired by progressive Asians, was opposed by the traditionally minded majority. It was pushed through by the Russian communists with a ruthlessness which neither Imperial Russia nor any other earlier colonial power would have attempted. The redistribution of land, in principle desired by the peasants, was carried out in such a way as largely to benefit immigrant farmers from European Russia: from the point of view of the Asians it looked as if the Imperial Russian policy was being continued. Imperial Russia, however, had always respected Islam in Central Asia. During the years of domination by the Tashkent 'poor white' Bolsheviks Islam had been actively persecuted. In the NEP years greater tolerance was shown, though the hostility of the regime to religion was never in doubt.

An extremely important aspect of Soviet policy in these years is the reorganisation of boundaries. Two Soviet republics were established—the Uzbek and the Turkmen—and three ASSR's within the Russian Soviet Federative Socialist Republic—the Kazakh, Kirgiz and Tadjik. The three ASSR's became full republics in the 1930's. The ostensible purpose of this reorganisation was to make the boundaries coincide with ethnical divisions. But in fact it is very questionable how precise these differences were. Certainly there were considerable differences between the dialects spoken by Turkmens, Uzbeks and Kirgiz, yet these were closely related to each other and could in 1921 hardly be described as distinct languages. Still more doubtful was their division into separate 'nations'. The Tadjiks differed from the others in that their language was not Turkic but Iranian, but it is doubtful whether they could be considered a separate nation, rather than a branch of the Persian nation. The clear purpose of Soviet policy was to destroy any feeling of a common Turkestani, or Turkic, or Persian nationality or culture. It was to manufacture a number of different nations, which could be kept apart from each other, played off against each other, and linked individually with the Russian nation. Thus any danger of a common front of the Central Asian Moslems could be removed. This policy of 'divide and rule' was of course no communist invention: it had been practised by both ancient and modern empires in both Europe and Asia.

* * *

In the 1930's collectivisation of agriculture and the forced development of heavy industry placed terrible burdens on all the citizens of the Soviet Union. It was especially severe in Ukraine and in the Kazakh steppes. The Ukrainian peasants, who lacked the tradition of the village commune which was so strong among Russian peasants, were determined to keep their private small holdings. In some cases Red Army units had to be sent into the villages to enforce collectivisation and to collect the grain deliveries laid down by the planning authorities in Moscow. Large areas remained uncultivated, and thousands of livestock were slaughtered. In 1932 and 1933 there were serious crop shortages and in 1933 the government refused either to reduce its delivery quotas or to release reserves of grain from the state granaries. The result was a famine in the Ukraine and the Kuban region from which several million peasants died. In the Kazakh steppes the authorities sought arbitrarily to end the nomadic form of life which had prevailed in this region from time immemorial, and to force the Kazakhs into permanent agricultural settlement. The result was mass destruction of livestock and famine. About one third of the whole Kazakh people perished. Livestock losses were also exceptionally high in Central Asia. In Turkmenia the number of cattle in 1933 was just over a fifth of what it had been in 1929; in Kirgizia in 1934 the number of sheep and goats was less than a quarter of the number in 1927–1928.

The bitterness caused by economic hardship naturally stimulated anti-Russian nationalism, and made the Soviet government ever more suspicious of the nationalities. The communist parties of the republics were heavily purged. The most important case was the Ukraine. In 1930 a group of non-communist intellectuals were tried in Kharkov on the charge of organising a secret 'League for the Liberation of Ukraine'. In 1933 the Ukrainian Commissar of Education, N. A. Skrypnik, who in the preceding decade had been the most active champion of 'Ukrainianisation', and had powerfully protected Ukrainian literature, art and science, committed suicide, and power passed into the hands of reliable exponents of Stalin's policies: during 1933 more than half the officials of the Ukrainian party machine were replaced. In the Tatar ASSR too there was a purge. After his disgrace in 1923 Sultan-Galiev had been allowed to earn his living as a private citizen. In 1929 he was arrested and disappeared. Tatar communists or officials suspected of 'Sultan-Galievism', that is, of Tatar patriotism or pan-Turkic ideas, were removed from their posts and in some cases arrested.

* * *

The Great Purge of 1936–1939 swept away hundreds of thousands of leading non-Russian communists. In the Ukraine all members of the republican Politburo and the republican Council of People's Commissars, and four-fifths of the members of the republican Central Committee of the Communist Party disappeared from public life. There were drastic purges in White Russia, in the three Transcaucasian republics and in the smaller regions—for instance in the Tatar, Daghestan, Mountaineers' and Buryat Mongol ASSR's. In Central Asia the still small number of communist officials of Asian origin was greatly reduced. The two best-known of them, Faizulla Hodzhaev and Akbal Ikramov, respectively Prime Minister and First Secretary of the Communist Party in the Uzbek republic, were among the accused at the show trial of March 1938, whose chief defendant was Bukharin, and both men were shot. Of the vast number of less eminent victims of the purges, many were executed or perished as a result of torture, while the majority disappeared in the concentration camps of the north and east. Some emerged still alive in the 1950's.

The Great Purge had just spent its force when the Second World War began in Europe. This was used by Stalin as an opportunity to expand the frontiers of his empire. By the Fifth Partition of Poland, between the Soviet Union and the Nazi Third Reich, the share of the former was the eastern half of Poland, the majority of whose population consisted of Ukrainians or White Russians, though several million Poles also lived there. Stalin's agreement with Hitler also recognised that the Baltic states and Finland lay in the Soviet sphere. In the winter of 1939–1940 the Soviet Union made war on Finland, which was obliged to cede the districts of Vyborg, on the Gulf of Finland near Leningrad, and Petsamo, on the Arctic coast. The three Baltic states were first compelled only to accept Red Army garrisons at certain strategic points. In June 1940, however, the Soviet leader decided to annex them. The Red Army marched in, puppet governments were set up under communist control, and after the ceremony of 'elections' without opposition candidates the 'parliaments' solemnly asked the Soviet government to accept their countries within the Soviet Union. They duly became the Lithuanian, Latvian and Estonian Soviet Socialist Republics. During the following months tens of thousands of citizens, especially Protestant clergy and members of the free professions, were deported into the interior of Russia. At the end of June 1940 the Soviet Union annexed Bessarabia from Roumania, thereby achieving an aim which it had never even formally abandoned. It also added the northern part of Bukovina, which had never belonged to the Russian Empire, but had a predominantly Ukrainian population. Thus almost all Ukrainians, and all White Russians, were now within the Soviet frontiers. From the national point of view this was a gain, though it is doubtful whether the form of government to which the new citizens were subjected gave them much pleasure. From the Soviet point of view the annexation had the great merit of destroying the possibility of Ukrainian or White Russian national movements being directed against the Soviet Union from foreign territory with a Ukrainian or White Russian population.

* * *

The outbreak of war with Hitler's Reich in June 1941 was in part brought about by Soviet attempts to obtain still further territorial gains—in the Black Sea Straits—and a further sphere of influence—in Bulgaria. Hitler was in any case resolved at some time to attack Russia, but the unashamed imperial greed of Stalin and Molotov, revealed in the diplomatic negotiations of 1940–1941, possibly accelerated his plans.

During the war the distrust of non-Russians by the Soviet government was even greater. Stalin's solution was to deport whole nations from their homelands, and to 'resettle' those who survived the journey in Siberia and Central Asia. The first victims were the 400,000 Germans of the Volga, who had been settled there since the mid-eighteenth century and had formed an ASSR since 1924. In 1944 the same fate befell the Crimean Tatars, the Kalmyks of the Caspian steppes and four nations of the Caucasus—the Chechens, Ingush, Balkars and Karachays. These groups together numbered about one and a half million persons. In the case of the Chechens, of which there are some eye-witness accounts, many persons were killed while being rounded up by security police forces, and it is probable that more perished during their transportation in the bitter Russian winter. The grounds given for the 1944 deportations were that these peoples had shown insufficient support of the Soviet war effort, that some of their number had helped the advancing German army, and that the majority had not denounced or punished these 'traitors to the Soviet Union'. It is doubtful whether the Germans received significant aid from them, but it is certain that the Caucasian mountain peoples had never been reconciled to Russian rule, and likely that in the war they saw an opportunity to liberate themselves by armed revolt.

The Soviet communists, who are never tired of posing as

defenders of national liberation movements against 'imperialism', treated the nationalism of the Caucasian peoples as a crime. In Burma during the Second World War a minority of the population actively assisted the invading Japanese, and the majority of the Burmese people certainly took no action against these people. If the British, on returning to Burma in 1945, had followed the example of the 'anti-imperialist' Soviet government, they would not only have executed those who served in the Burmese National Army, but would have deported the whole of the Burmese people to Arctic Canada.

In 1944–1945 the Red Army drove the Germans back to Berlin. In the subsequent peace settlement, Soviet rule was re-established in the portions of Finland, Poland and Roumania annexed in 1939–1940, and the Baltic States were reincorporated. The Soviet Union also annexed Transcarpathian Ruthenia, the one province of Ukrainian population still outside its grasp, which had been part of Hungary from the Middle Ages until 1918, had passed to Czechoslovakia in 1918, and had returned to Hungary in 1939. It also annexed half of East Prussia, with its ancient German capital of Königsberg, now renamed Kaliningrad. In the Far East the Soviet Union annexed the southern half of Sakhalin, which the Russian Empire had ceded to Japan in 1905, and the Kurile Islands, which Russia had recognised as Japanese in 1875. In 1944 the People's Republic of Tannu Tuva was formally incorporated in the Soviet Union.

The Soviet Union was thus the only Great Power to make territorial gains as a result of the war. In the following years the European Great Powers and the United States gave independence to scores or hundreds of millions of colonial subjects, but the Soviet Union has kept all its conquests.

* * *

In the post-war years the Soviet leaders showed themselves especially fearful of external influences undermining the communist regime. They were extremely suspicious of 'bourgeois nationalism' among the non-Russians. There were numerous changes in leading personnel in the Ukraine and in the Asian republics, in which accusations of nationalism were made. In the official doctrine, there were two great sins—nationalism and cosmopolitanism—and two great virtues—patriotism and internationalism. A non-Russian citizen of the Soviet Union was guilty of nationalism if he stressed the differences that separated his nation from the Russian nation, of cosmopolitanism if he stressed cultural links between his nation and any nation living outside the Soviet Union. For example, Uzbeks and Tadjiks must not stress the common cultural tradition of Arabic and Persian literature, which they shared with the people of Persia, Turkey or the Arab lands. Patriotism must be always on behalf of the Soviet Union. A patriot must insist on the superiority of the Soviet Union to neighbouring countries, and must even put forward territorial claims against neighbour states. For example, a Georgian patriot must seek not independence for Georgia, but the incorporation in the Georgian SSR of Turkish territories that were once Georgian, or which have some inhabitants of Georgian speech (Lazistan, in north-east Turkey). Azerbaidjanis must of course seek the incorporation in the Soviet Union of Persian Azerbaidjan (which was occupied by Soviet troops in 1945–1946). Internationalism, which is in the Soviet view fully compatible with patriotism, requires constant emphasis on solidarity between one's own people and the Russian people, indeed servility towards the Russian people and Russian culture.

These principles were even extended into the past. The traditional epic poems of the Turkic peoples were denounced because they revealed a 'nationalistic' spirit. Soviet historians, who hitherto had denounced the conquest by the Tsars of the Caucasus and Central Asia as acts of imperialism, were now obliged to praise it, and to denounce the leaders of resistance to the Imperial Russian armies as agents of British or Turkish imperialism. The hero of Daghestan in the first half of the nineteenth century, Imam Shamil, was now presented as a reactionary *mulla* and Anglo-Turkish puppet. The conquests of the Tsars were praised as objectively progressive, for two main reasons: because they accelerated the necessary social development of these nations from 'feudalism' to 'capitalism', and because they brought them into contact with the superior culture of the Russian people. There is of course some truth in these arguments, just as much and just as little as in the argument that British and French colonial rule assisted the modernisation of India and Indo-China, and that the Indians and Indo-Chinese benefited from British and French cultural influence. The arguments of the Soviet historians are in fact a quasi-Marxist version of the doctrine of 'the white man's burden'. Kipling would have understood what they meant.

* * *

The death of Stalin brought a much milder policy. The non-Russians of course benefited from the reduction of police terror, the disbandment of most of the concentration camps, the repeal of some penal legislation, the improved prices for farm produce and the increased production of consumer goods which combined to make life much more pleasant for Soviet citizens at the end of the 1950's. N. S. Khrushchov, who had served for eleven years in the Ukraine, took some trouble, once he had risen to first place among the Soviet leaders, to flatter Ukrainian national feeling. In 1954 the tercentenary of the union of Pereyaslavl was celebrated with some pomp, and it was made clear that if the Russians were the elder brother in the Soviet family of nations, the Ukrainians were the second brother. Khrushchov promoted a large number of Ukrainians to high government and party posts in Moscow and in Russia. The disgrace of Beria, the Georgian-born chief of the security police, and of his close associate in Azerbaidjan, M. D. Bagirov, made possible a turnover of personnel in Transcaucasia which gave new men their chance of a career. In Georgia, however, the discrediting of Stalin in Khrushchov's 'secret session' speech at the 20th Congress of the CPSU in February 1956 caused indignation which expressed itself in large-scale riots. It appears that angry Stalinists and Georgian nationalists for a time joined forces. In Central Asia there was less denunciation of 'bourgeois nationalism'. For the first time a Central Asian, N. A. Mukhitdinov of the Uzbek SSR, became (in 1957) a member of the highest political organ of the Soviet Union, the Presidium of the Central Committee of the Communist Party. In the Baltic states greater power was given to Baltic communists, and Russians became less prominent.

* * *

In the light of this brief survey of the development of 'nationality policy' since 1921, we must now consider certain broad aspects of the relationship between Russians and non-Russians in the Soviet Union—the structure of political power, economic development, education and culture.

The Soviet Constitution is sometimes described as 'federal'. This is a mistake. Federal government implies the distribution of powers between the central and regional authorities, with each supreme in certain fields. This is not the case in the Soviet Union. The fifteen SSR's are not co-ordinate with the central government, but subordinate to it. The Soviet Union has a unitary form of government, with some decentralisation or devolution of authority to the republics. Even this decentralisation is modified by the fact that the Communist Party, which controls the whole apparatus of government, is highly centralised. Under the Constitution, the republics have the right to secede from the Union. But any person who advocated secession would make himself guilty of 'counter-revolutionary propaganda', which is severely punished under the Soviet criminal code.

Government in the republics and ASSR's, like government at the centre, is a dictatorship by the Communist Party. But in the non-Russian regions, this dictatorship is to varying extents administered by members of the non-Russian peoples. In the Ukraine it seems that most important posts are held by Ukrainians, though this cannot be very easily determined from a study of names of officials, since Russian and Ukrainian names are not easily distinguished, and even bearers of distinctly Ukrainian names may be Russian in speech and outlook (as, for example, a man named Mackenzie whose family has lived for generations in England may be indistinguishable in all important respects from his English neighbour named Smith). In Georgia and Armenia it seems that Georgians and Armenians are in command, and in Azerbaidjan the number of Russians in public posts does not appear to exceed the proportion of Russians in the population of the republic. In Central Asia Russians undoubtedly hold a great deal of power. The highest posts are normally held by Asians, while their seconds-in-command are Russians. Thus, the normal pattern is that the First Secretary of the republican party central committee, and the first secretaries of provincial party committees within the republic, are Asians, while the second secretaries at both levels are Russians. Again, the Prime Minister of the republic is normally an Asian, while one of the Deputy Prime Ministers is a Russian. Republican ministers are mostly Asians, while the heads of departments in the ministries are often Russians.

* * *

The Soviet Union has become the second industrial power in the world. This tremendous economic progress, part of whose foundations were laid in the Imperial period, has of course in some measure benefited all Soviet citizens, whether Russian or not. As we have seen, the main grain and mineral resources are found outside the main area of Russian population. These have been developed for the benefit of the state as a whole, rather than for the benefit of the peoples in whose lands the resources lie. Certainly these peoples too have benefited, and it is even arguable that direction of the whole economy from one centre has given them better results than they would have had if they had had independent states. Certainly independent states of Azerbaidjan, Georgia or Turkestan would not have conducted their economic policy in the same way.

The development of these resources has of course brought an enormous influx of Russians (and also of Ukrainians) into the industrial centres, and to some extent into the countryside. The Urals were a mining centre, as we have seen, already in the eighteenth century. In the nineteenth, they were far surpassed in production by the Ukraine. It was not until the Soviet period that the government paid great attention to this region. As a result of the first two Five Year Plans, and still more of the evacuation of factories and workers during the German invasion of European Russia in 1941, the Urals have become one of the greatest centres of metallurgical and engineering industry in the world. The coal resources of the Kuznets Basin in Siberia have also formed the base for a large metallurgical industry. In both these great industrial areas the original Bashkir, Tatar or minor Siberian peoples have been swamped by the influx of Russians. The same has happened in the oil-bearing regions. Baku is largely a Russian city, though the Azeri element in its population and in its working class is considerable. In the Bashkir republic already in the 1920's the Bashkirs formed only a quarter of the population, and the development in this region of the second main oil industry of the Soviet Union, from the 1930's onwards, has led as inexorably to the disappearance of Bashkir civilisation in Russia as the discovery of oil in Oklahoma to the absorption of the Oklahoma Red Indians by white American civilisation.

*　　*　　*

Agricultural colonisation by Russian peasants in the Kazakh steppes and Turkestan, begun by the Imperial regime, has been continued in the Soviet Union. In the Kazakh SSR Russians formed in 1959 52% of the population, in the Kirgiz SSR 37%, in the Turkmen SSR 18% and in the Uzbek SSR and the Tadjik SSR 15% each. The development of Khrushchov's plans for the cultivation of the

68

'virgin lands' of Kazakhstan will inevitably increase the Russian majority in that republic.

The concentration of agricultural effort on specialised crops, also begun by the Imperial regime, has also continued. Tea production in Georgia is an example. Still more important is cotton production in Turkestan. Five times as much cotton is grown in this region as before the Revolution, and it now supplies 85% of the raw material for the Soviet cotton textile industry. Yields per unit of land are much higher than in the past, but are capable of further improvement. This specialisation is not popular with all Uzbek communists. There have from time to time been attempts to diversify agriculture in Central Asia, but these have been successfully resisted by Moscow. The needs of the whole Soviet economy must, it is argued, come before the preferences of the people of one area. If Turkestan were independent, it would certainly not make its economy so utterly dependent on a single crop. But to think in terms of the needs of Turkestan alone is to commit the sin of 'bourgeois nationalism'. The analogy between the Soviet insistence on cotton in Turkestan and the British forced development of cotton in Egypt is striking.

Industry has also been developed in the Asian republics. In Central Asia, for example, there are factories for the manufacture of fertilisers and of spinning machinery, as well as some types of engineering and a fairly wide range of consumer-goods industries. A survey carried out in 1957 by the United Nations Economic Commission for Europe estimated that living standards in the Uzbek, Turkmen, Tadjik and Kirgiz republics were only 20–25% below the level for the Soviet Union as a whole. As the Commission pointed out, a regional disparity of living standards on this scale is quite common in most countries of Europe. There can be no doubt that the material conditions of the people of the Soviet Central Asian republics are substantially better than those of the neighbouring countries, Persia and Afghanistan.

*   *   *

Great progress has certainly been made also in education. The general approach of the Soviet government to education was diametrically opposed to that of the Tsars. Whereas Imperial ministers of education feared to educate the masses because this might put ideas into their heads, the Soviet leaders (like the reformers in Japan in the Meiji Era) believed that educated boys and girls would be more efficient workers, peasants and soldiers than uneducated. During the Soviet era, and especially from the mid-1930's onwards, education at all levels has made rapid progress, and the quality has also greatly improved, particularly in the last ten years. This has benefited Russians and non-Russians alike. Even in Central Asia it is now claimed that 90% of the population is literate. Though the proportion must certainly be lower than this for the Asian population alone (about 7,000,000 out of 24,000,000 inhabitants of the whole area are Russians), it is still an impressive achievement. It is also true that education in primary and secondary schools is largely conducted in the Asian languages, and that there is a vast output of books and periodicals in these languages. The content of this literature is of course subject to the same limitation as applies to all literature in the Soviet Union—that it may not criticise the policy of the Communist Party, and may not even diverge from the principles laid down by the party in regard to non-political matters.

It must, however, be recognised that this development of education has been designed to serve not the individual cultures of the non-Russian peoples but a synthetic Soviet communist culture, and that this Soviet culture in practice contains strong elements of Russification. The Islamic element in the cultures of the Tatars, Azeris, Caucasians and Central Asians is being as far as possible eradicated. The development of standardised literary languages for the separate 'nations' of Central Asia was so conducted as to remove as many Arabic and Persian words as possible, and to introduce Russian words, and even to remodel grammar and syntax on Russian lines. In the 1920's Soviet policy was to replace the Arabic alphabet by variants of the Latin alphabet (as was done at the same period in Turkey by Kemal Atatürk). This effectively cut off the younger generation from their traditional culture. But from the end of the 1930's it was decided to replace the Latin alphabets by modified Cyrillic alphabets, thus cutting young people off from Europe and from Turkey. Much greater emphasis was also laid on the teaching of Russian in the schools of the non-Russian regions. It is of course not unreasonable that young people should be expected to learn the language of the most numerous and most advanced nation in the Union. Knowledge of Russian is as useful to young Azeris or Tadjiks or Yakuts as knowledge of English is useful to young Bengalis or Madrasis. But the imperfect information available suggests that in practice the proportion of children receiving their education in Russian is considerably higher than the proportion of Russians in the population. This is particularly the case in universities and institutes of higher education. There are also grounds for believing that among the university and higher level technical students in the Central Asian republics and Azerbaidjan a rather high proportion are Russians. This is still more the case with the teaching staff. The outstanding exceptions to this statement are the republics of Georgia and Armenia. Here the traditional national alphabets are in use, and there is strong (even obstinately chauvinist) opposition to the use of Russian.

Thus the economic and cultural achievements of the Soviet regime in the non-Russian regions are great, and deserve credit. But the advantages which these nations enjoy were handed down to them from above, by a government which was convinced that it knew their interests much better than they themselves. This is a paternalist attitude, typical of imperial and colonial regimes. The Soviet empire, like the British and French empires, has its benevolent as well as its repressive aspects. It may be that the material achievements of the Soviet empire are greater than those of the British empire, but they were achieved at the cost of deliberately uprooting the native Islamic culture, with a savage doctrinaire intolerance of which neither the British in India nor the French in Algeria were capable. Whether on balance this has been to the advantage of the Russian Moslems is a matter on which different opinions are possible. As for the repressive aspects, these include the deliberate starving to death of millions of Ukrainian peasants and Kazakh nomads and the deportation of whole nations from their homes, actions beside which the British reprisals after the Indian Mutiny of 1857 or French repression of Algerian rebels in the 1950's seem comparatively mild.

* * *

It is often pointed out that there is no 'colour-bar' in the Soviet Union. Discrimination based on physical characteristics of race is hardly conceivable, for the physical types of Russian, Tatar and Turkestani merge imperceptibly into each other. There has never been in Russia a direct confrontation between utterly different racial types, as in colonial Africa or the American South. It appears, however, from the recent experience of African and dark-skinned Asian students in Moscow that Russians do not show themselves as racially tolerant in practice as they proclaim in theory. Even sexual taboo has made its ugly appearance.

But if in Central Asia there is no colour-bar this does not mean that Russians and Asians freely mix. Most cities of Central Asia have in practice separate residential areas for Russians and Asians (Alma Ata and Stalinabad appear to be exceptions). In ministerial offices and factories the two groups meet and work together. But in their private social lives they do not meet, and intermarriage is very rare. As in other mixed societies, it seems that social intercourse and tolerance are most frequent in the upper strata—high officials and intellectuals—and least practised lower down the social pyramid—by 'poor whites' or *petits blancs*. Here the analogies with the United States or with European colonies are obvious.

The Soviet government has set itself the task of creating an overriding Soviet patriotism and sense of a Soviet nation. It is impossible to estimate with certainty how successful it has been. A parallel is sometimes made with the American case. In the plains of Minnesota or the factories of Pittsburgh, and in the school system of the whole United States, boys and girls of Irish or German or Slovak or Italian origin were formed into Americans. It might be supposed that Sverdlovsk, Tashkent and Kharkov are similar melting-pots, from which a Soviet nation is emerging. It may be so. But it should not be forgotten that the problems facing the Soviet authorities in this respect are greater than those which faced the American. The United States from its inception had a legal and cultural framework, into which the immigrants were fitted, and the immigrants had left their homeland to arrive in America. But in the Soviet Union the non-Russian peoples are living in compact communities in their traditional homelands. They may be acquiring a new loyalty to the Soviet Union, in place of their previous rancorous submission to a Russian conqueror (though this is by no means sure). But they will hardly cease to be Uzbeks or Ukrainians, as the people of Detroit have ceased to be Poles or Italians.

*　　*　　*

Soviet education has created numerous new strata of modern outlook among the non-Russian peoples—in Soviet terminology, new 'people's *intelligentsia*'. The Soviet leaders rely on them to be the most active propagators among their peoples of the Soviet system of values. Their expectations may be fulfilled. But, to say the least, it is uncertain. The British in India and the French in Indo-China made it possible for a certain number of their subjects to acquire a modern education. Without the British and French conquests they would not have had this opportunity. In the pre-1914 Kingdom of Hungary, under Habsburg rule, Slovaks and Serbs and Roumanians who learned the Hungarian (Magyar) language could obtain an excellent education at the university of Budapest. Jawaharlal Nehru and Ho Chi-minh could hold their own with the flower of the British or French cultural elite. Slovak and Roumanian and Serbian intellectuals fully absorbed all that Hungary had to give them in literature, art or *douceur de vivre*. But these men did not become exponents among their own peoples of the alien rule. On the contrary, they used the knowledge and skill which their education had given them to lead nationalist movements against Britain, France and Hungary.

Has the Soviet regime found some miraculous formula for curing the new *intelligentsia* of nationalism? Or is the absence of Georgian or Uzbek equivalents of the Indian National Congress due simply to the one-party regime of the Communist Party and the powers of the Soviet security police?

In 1956 it was shown that communism has no miraculous cure. The intellectual youth of Hungary were children of workers and peasants who had received a higher education in the preceding ten years as a result of the policy of the communist government, which had thrown open the universities and colleges to those who had been excluded from them under the old regime. Yet it was this intellectual youth which led the national resistance against a regime which was hateful not only for its cruel methods of government but above all because it was the creation of a foreign invader.

In view of the past experience of all colonial empires, and the role played by the *intelligentsia* in so many countries of Asia and Africa in the last decades, it would be astounding if the *intelligentsia* of the non-Russian nations of the Soviet Union were not affected by nationalism, did not cherish the hope that one day they may achieve independence.

5

The Soviet Satellites

WITH their victory in civil war in Russia, the task of the
Soviet communists had only begun. Russia was the first
country in which a communist party was in power, but the
aim was not a communist Russia but a communist world.
The laws of history, as established by Marxist science, laid
down that the human race was bound to pass through successive stages to socialism, and through socialism to communism. But communists must not sit back and let history
do their job for them: they must put all their effort into
the acceleration of the process. This had always been Lenin's
firm belief. Passive trusting to 'elemental' forces had been in
his view one of the gravest sins of which a communist was
capable. The *raison d'être* of a communist government
was to help on world-wide revolution. The only limitation
was that the base itself must not be endangered by fool-
hardy action. Russian communists must clearly consolidate
their power in Russia, and build up a socialist order in
Russia. But they must also help revolution, both in industrial Europe (where they placed their main hopes) and in
backward Asia.

Help included military help if and when it could be
useful, as in Poland in the summer of 1920 and in Mongolia in the spring of 1921. But certainly Lenin did not
think of world socialist revolution as primarily a process
of military conquest by the Red Army. In Europe he believed that the main effort would be made by the European
workers themselves. In Asia he regarded such help as the
Red Army could give as being the very antithesis of imperialism. The Red Army might help Asians to throw off
the yoke of European imperialists. There could be no

question of Soviet Russia carrying out an imperialism of her own. He deplored the excesses of the Tashkent Bolsheviks against the Turkestan Moslems, and he was unhappy about the invasion of Georgia, and still more about the methods of Stalin in setting up a Bolshevik regime there. His view of the invasion of Mongolia is not known: perhaps he had not learned much about its consequences by the time that illness laid him low. But the cases of Turkestan and Georgia seemed to him no more than lamentable aberrations from a basically sound policy. As the evil habits of mind created by centuries of 'feudalism' and 'capitalism' wore off, a free and just society would emerge.

The hopes of revolution in Europe receded after 1919. To Lenin's successors the main task was the creation of a new regime in Russia. One of the main subjects of disagreement between Stalin and his rivals for the succession to Lenin was whether or not socialism could be built in one country. The complexities of this controversy cannot concern us here. It suffices to say that Stalin, the victor, never abandoned the aim of world revolution: he only gave it a lower temporary priority than Trotski or Zinoviev had done. Though socialism could, he claimed, be built in the Soviet Union alone, it would never be secure as long as it was threatened by 'capitalist encirclement'. Only when several of the advanced industrial countries of the world had socialist governments could the Soviet system be safe, and 'the complete victory of socialism' be assured.

But as a result of the great changes which took place in the Soviet Union after Stalin's 'second revolution' of 1929, the content of the word 'socialism' itself underwent change. In 1936 a new Constitution was introduced in the Soviet Union. It stated that the Soviet Union was 'a socialist state of workers and peasants'. The new order created by forced collectivisation of agriculture and forced planned industrialisation *was* socialism. The Soviet regime had become a blueprint for socialism. Nothing else was socialism. Socialists were people whose aim was the establishment in their countries of a system modelled on the Soviet blueprint.

Socialist parties were Marxist-Leninist parties, accepting the current party line as expounded at any particular moment by the orthodox ideologists in Moscow. Parties which called themselves socialist, but did not accept the party line, or did not even profess Marxism-Leninism—for example, the British Labour Party or the German Social Democratic Party—were not socialist at all. Socialist revolution could only mean the extension by force of the Soviet system to other countries.

* * *

Before the Second World War the implications of these principles were not obvious. The only country in which they could be carried out was Mongolia. From 1929 to 1932 a 'left' policy of 'socialist transformation' was pursued, which provoked widespread resistance and economic chaos. After this more moderate policies were pursued. In 1938 the Soviet purges were imitated in Mongolia: their victims were persons suspected of Mongolian nationalism, that is, of a desire to make their country less dependent on the Soviet Union. The undisputed satrap of Mongolia, its 'little Stalin', was Marshal Choibalsan, who had survived his former comrades of 1921. In 1949 a constitution was adopted which barely differed from that of the Buryat Mongol ASSR of the Soviet Union. The Mongolian economy was closely tied to that of the Soviet Union. In 1941 a Cyrillic alphabet was introduced for the Mongol language, replacing the Latin alphabet which had been introduced in 1931 to replace the traditional Mongol script. By the time of Choibalsan's death in 1952 the Mongolian People's Republic was a satellite of the Soviet Union, differing from the Soviet republics only in its more backward economy.

The development of the Mongolian satellite was, however, little known in the outside world. It was not until the occupation by the Soviet army of half of Europe in 1944–1945 that the significance of the new conceptions of 'socialism' and 'socialist revolution' became better understood.

* * *

Pursuing the defeated German armies, Soviet forces re-occupied the Baltic states, eastern Poland and Bessarabia; occupied the rest of Poland, part of Germany, all Czechoslovakia, Hungary, Roumania and Bulgaria; and passed through the north-eastern corner of Yugoslavia. In the Far East they occupied all Manchuria and the northern half of Korea.

In occupied Germany and Korea the Soviet authorities set up, by stages, regimes controlled by communist parties and based on the Soviet model. The presence of Soviet troops in Manchuria was of some importance in providing the Chinese communists with arms to win their civil war against the armies of Chiang Kai-shek, but the Soviet army was fairly soon withdrawn from all Chinese territory except the Liaotung peninsula, ceded to the Soviet Union by the treaty of 1945 between the Soviet government and the government of Chiang Kai-shek. This too was restored to Communist China ten years later.

In Yugoslavia the communists themselves seized power as a result of a long war fought both against the German invaders and against Yugoslav political forces, both fascist and democratic. In Albania too the communists seized power by their own efforts, with some aid from the Yugoslavs.

We shall here concern ourselves neither with the two areas of complete Soviet occupation (East Germany and North Korea) nor with the two countries of native communist regimes (Yugoslavia and Albania), though we shall have occasion to mention them from time to time. The subject of this chapter is the five European satellites, where communists were put in power essentially by Soviet action, but which preserved at least the appearance of independent united states. These are Poland, Czechoslovakia, Hungary, Roumania and Bulgaria.

Until they incurred the common fate of being subjected to communist rule, the peoples of these five countries were more remarkable for the differences between them than for the similarities. Poles, Czechs, Slovaks and Bulgarians speak languages of the Slav group, closely related to Russian, while the Roumanian language is predominantly Latin and the Hungarian is completely different from any other spoken in Europe. Poles, Czechs, Slovaks and Hungarians are mostly Catholic by religion, Roumanians and Bulgarians are Orthodox, while there are important Protestant minorities in Slovakia and Hungary and a large Moslem minority in Bulgaria. In 1945 the Czech lands had a predominantly industrial economy, in Poland and Hungary industry and agriculture were fairly evenly balanced, while Slovakia, Roumania and Bulgaria were overwhelmingly agrarian countries.

All six nations had spent long periods of their history under foreign rule (Austrian, Prussian, Russian or Turkish). Those which had had the longest record of state independence were the Poles and Hungarians. The only nation which had a strong tradition of political democracy were the Czechs: the Czechoslovak Republic of 1918–1938 was a genuinely free and socially progressive parliamentary state. In Poland and Hungary the traditional form of government was oligarchy, which was at times liberal and at times dictatorial. Roumania and Bulgaria in the years after the First World War usually had dictatorial governments. The strongest communist party in the region before 1945 was the Czechoslovak, which was supported by about half the Czech working class. In Bulgaria the communist party, though small and persecuted, was well organised and bravely led. In the other three countries communism was a negligible force.

* * *

In 1944–1945 the Soviet army fought the Germans in Poland. Under German rule the Polish resistance movement had built up a brave and efficient underground army and indeed a more or less complete underground state, civil as well as military. The leaders of this movement offered their help to the Soviet army. They were arrested for their pains, and the Soviet authorities ruthlessly destroyed the Polish underground state. In its place they set up a 'government' of Polish communists imported from Russia. After some months of fruitless protestation and argument, the American and British governments recognised this 'government', on condition that representatives of the democratic Polish emigration in the West should be included in it, and that free elections be held. But in practice the returning democratic exiles were denied any effective political influence, and there were no free elections. The Polish communists set up their own dictatorship under protection of the Soviet army.

Roumania and Bulgaria had been allied to Germany, and the Roumanian army had taken part in Hitler's war on the Soviet Union. In August 1944 King Michael of Roumania brought his country out of the war, and in the following winter the Roumanian army fought on the Soviet side against the Germans. Two weeks later there was a revolution in Bulgaria, and the Bulgarian army also joined the war on the Soviet side. In both countries coalition governments were formed in which the communists took part together with the peasant parties and socialist parties. The organisation of the armies and the apparatus of civil government were left more or less intact until the war with Germany was over. Then, with strong Soviet support, the communists set about purging them and replacing the dismissed officers and officials with their own nominees. In Hungary and Czechoslovakia, at the time of the defeat of the Germans, the machinery of government had almost ceased to exist. Here too coalition governments of communists, socialists, liberal democrats and peasant parties were set up, and the apparatus of civil power was reconstructed. The Soviet army was withdrawn from Czechoslovakia in December 1945. Elsewhere it remained—in Hungary, Roumania and Bulgaria because they were defeated enemy countries, in Poland on the ground that it needed direct communications with its army of occupation in Germany.

*　　*　　*

The seizure of complete power by the communists in these five countries took place between 1945 and 1948. In general three stages may be distinguished. In the first, government was by a genuine coalition, in which the non-communist parties enjoyed freedom of organisation, comparative freedom of speech, and put forward their own policies. In the second stage genuine coalitions were replaced by bogus coalitions, in which the leaders and policies of the non-communist parties were chosen not by their own members but by the communist leaders, and in which no spokesman of these parties might criticise communist policy. In this stage opposition could still be expressed from outside the government, by socialist or peasant party leaders who had been forced out of their own parties by a communist-staged purge. In the third stage the remnants of the non-communist parties were either abolished or turned into completely docile 'front organisations' of the communist party, and all opposition outside the government ranks was suppressed. In Poland the first stage never occurred at all: the regime of the communist puppet government including a few helpless returned exiles, as set up in 1945, was a regime of the second stage. In Roumania and Bulgaria the first stage lasted only till the spring or early summer of 1945. In Hungary it lasted until the spring of 1947, in Czechoslovakia until February 1948. By the end of 1948 all five countries had reached the third stage.

The communists owed their victory partly to a systematic policy of placing their men in key positions in the civil and military bureaucracy, and of bribing or blackmailing officials of the old regime to support them against their democratic rivals. They paid particular attention to the police (especially to the security and counter-espionage departments), to the armed forces (especially to the counter-intelligence in the general staffs), and to the means of publicity (especially to broadcasting). They also placed their men in the management of factories which, by the agreed policy of the coalitions, were nationalised, and they controlled the trade unions, which were rapidly expanded. The communists on the whole possessed a better understanding of the realities of power than their opponents. Yet even this superior skill would not have given them victory, in view of the very small popular support which they enjoyed in four out of the five countries, had they not received constant and powerful backing from the Soviet occupation forces. In all five countries, in the first chaotic months after 'liberation' from the Germans, the Soviet military commanders and their political advisers, at various levels, intervened to place communists, or men recommended by communists, in important posts, or made available to the communist parties material resources with which they were able to attract recruits, while hampering the movements of the democrats and at times victimising them on false charges of having 'collaborated' with the Germans. In Poland they brutally eliminated the leaders and the middle ranks of the Polish national movement. In Roumania in February 1945 the Soviet Foreign Minister, A. Y. Vyshinski, forced King Michael to appoint an unrepresentative, communist-controlled government by a direct threat of Soviet military action. In Bulgaria at about the same time the Soviet commanding general forced the Agrarian Union to expel its most popular and courageous leader, Dr. G. M. Dimitrov. In Hungary in February 1947 the outstanding leader of the Small Farmers' Party, Béla Kovács, was arrested by Soviet security forces and deported to Russia. These actions were decisive in breaking the resistance of all four peoples.

The case of the fifth country, Czechoslovakia, is more complex. Here the Soviet army gave great help to the communists between May and December 1945, but then withdrew. In May 1946 a free parliamentary election was held, at which the communists emerged as the strongest single party, with nearly 40% of the poll. For nearly two years they behaved in a comparatively constitutional manner, and Czechoslovakia was rapidly becoming a democratic state, based on the rule of law, as it had been from 1918 to 1938. Nevertheless the communists held greater real power than appeared. In February 1948, partly because a new election was imminent in which they were certainly going to win fewer votes, and partly because of the general international situation (refusal by the Soviet Union of the Marshall Plan and creation of the Cominform), they decided to force a crisis and seize power. Their opponents made tactical mistakes which enabled the communists to get control of the Social Democratic Party and to browbeat the Head of State, President Eduard Beneš, and so to form a new government by constitutional means. The presence of the Soviet Deputy Foreign Minister, Zorin, in Prague during the crisis suggests that the action was planned by Moscow, but this cannot be asserted with certainty. The communists mobilised armed detachments of workers in the main cities and made good use of their hold on the security police. The action must be described as part-revolutionary and part-constitutional, and its success attributed partly to the Czechoslovak communists' own efforts and partly to Soviet direction and help, from 1945 onwards.

*　　*　　*

The political system set up in the five East European satellite states was closely copied from that of the Soviet Union. The new regimes were known as 'people's democracies' rather than 'socialist republics', because only the seizure of power had been completed, and the tasks of 'building socialism' still lay ahead. But power was exercised by the communist parties in essentially the same way, and through essentially the same institutional framework, as in the Soviet Union. The Councils of Ministers, legislative assemblies, ministerial bureaucracies and courts of law were completely subordinated to the party, through the party members who held the key positions in them. The armies and police forces were in communist hands. The press, book publication and broadcasting were used by the party as means of propaganda to indoctrinate the whole population. The schools were regarded as a political weapon, to mould the minds of children and turn them against their parents. Conflict with the Christian churches and with Islam was inevitable.

Religious services were permitted, but religious influence was increasingly excluded from the schools, and various measures were taken to make it difficult for adult citizens to practise their religions. The leaders of the churches were accused of political activity against the regime. Some were publicly tried and condemned, others were removed from their posts and interned.

The communists introduced centralised economic planning, based on Soviet experience. Priority was given to heavy industry, and the cost was borne by forcing both workers and peasants to work at low real wages. The trade unions were means for mobilising industrial manpower and enforcing labour discipline. They were designed not to uphold the workers' interests against their employers, but to impose the will of the employer-state on the workers. An elaborate structure of welfare services was created, but its practical value to the workers depended on the decision of the communist party at each particular moment. At times the party, in its benevolent wisdom, handed out material concessions, at times it exhorted the workers to tighten their belts. There was no question of the workers influencing the leaders of trade unions or of the party. The peasants paid their share of the cost by compulsory deliveries of farm goods at artificially low prices, and the government then sold these to the consumers at a great profit. From 1949 onwards pressure was increased to make peasants enter collective farms. The means used varied from discriminatory taxation to physical force and arrests of unwilling farmers. The most rapid progress was made in Bulgaria, the least in Roumania.

* * *

Not only were the peoples of the five countries placed under regimes which were copies of the Soviet regime: their countries were controlled and exploited by the Soviet Union. The economic ministries, the police forces and the Armies had 'Soviet advisers' attached to them, who were empowered to intervene as they thought fit. Some of these men were Russian, others were Soviet citizens who had been born in the country—for instance, Bulgarians who had lived for twenty years in exile in the Soviet Union. The most striking example of all was Marshal Konstantin Rokossovski, an outstanding military leader of the Red Army in the Second World War, who had been born of Polish parents, and was in 1949 appointed Minister of War in Poland and became a member of the Politburo of the Polish communist party.

The communist parties themselves were organised exactly as the CPSU: their 'statutes' were virtual translations of the statute of the CPSU. In the late 1940's the 'cult of personality' was at its height, and each satellite party had to have its 'little Stalin' (Gottwald in Czechoslovakia, Rákosi in Hungary, Bierut in Poland, Dimitrov and then Chervenkov in Bulgaria, Gheorghiu-Dej in Roumania). The parties were also obliged to carry out purges on instructions from Moscow. The quarrel between the Soviet and Yugoslav communists in 1948, which led to the excommunication of Marshal Tito by the Cominform, was followed by a witch-hunt against 'nationalist deviationism' in the satellite parties. Suitable scapegoats were found, Rajk in Hungary, Kostov in Bulgaria, Clementis in Czechoslovakia, Patrashcanu in Roumania, Gomulka in Poland. The first four were executed, but Gomulka was fortunate in being merely dismissed from his jobs and for a time arrested in comparatively mild conditions. From the confused mixture of half-truths and lies which enveloped the trials of the first four it was clear that their main sin was that they had to some extent opposed, or at least criticised, the Soviet domination of their countries. The purges of 'Nationalists' in 1949–1950 were followed by further purges in 1951–1952, which were especially severe in Czechoslovakia and Hungary, and whose victims included a high proportion of Jews. They were clearly connected with the anti-semitic campaign in the Soviet Union in the last year of Stalin's life. The outstanding victim of this period was Slánský, the secretary general of the Czechoslovak Communist Party.

Between 1949 and 1952 half the members of the Central Committees of the Czechoslovak and the Hungarian communist parties disappeared.

The economic plans of the satellites in these years were designed to make each produce all the main branches of industry, and to make each separately dependent on the Soviet Union. There was a ridiculous amount of overlapping. Industries for which there were no favourable conditions had to be set up, at great cost, and maintained by importing raw materials or machinery from the Soviet Union at uneconomic prices. It would have been wiser to make each country specialise in those branches of industry for which it had an aptitude, or special advantages of raw materials or transportation. But any division of labour between the satellites was unwelcome to Stalin, as he feared that it might make for closer co-operation between satellites whose economic needs were partly complementary to each other. Whatever the economic advantages, this was politically inadmissible. The East European satellites—like the Central Asian republics in the 1930's—must be kept apart from each other but individually linked to Moscow. In trade relations with the Soviet Union, the satellites were forced to pay high prices for Soviet goods and accept absurdly low prices for their exports. The most striking case is Polish coal, which had to be sold to the Soviet Union at one-tenth of the price offered by Denmark in 1945 (which the Poles were obliged to refuse). Bulgarian rose-water, a valuable ingredient of perfumes, was sold to the Soviet Union at a low price, and then resold by the Soviet government at a handsome profit on world markets. A special case was the 'joint companies' set up in Hungary and Roumania. The Soviet 'contribution' consisted of enterprises in these countries which had been seized by the Soviet government on the ground that they were German property. The contribution of the Roumanian and Hungarian governments consisted of other enterprises in the same field. The companies were supposed to operate for the mutual advantage of the two countries, but in fact were managed by the Soviet government for its own profit. These countries included a monopoly of air transport in both countries and a substantial portion of the oil and timber industries in Roumania and of the bauxite industry in Hungary. Soviet economic domination of Eastern Europe in the last years of Stalin's life can only be described by the familiar Marxist phrase 'colonial exploitation'.

It is, however, interesting to note that Stalin does not ever seem to have intended to incorporate the East European States in the Soviet Union, as he had incorporated the Baltic States in 1940, and again in 1944–1945. The Baltic States differed from the East European States in that they had once been part of the Russian Empire. This curiously conservative and 'patriotic' attitude of the non-Russian Georgian Stalin, who considered himself the heir to the rightful estates of the Tsars, is shown in the seizure of Bessarabia (which was not returned to Roumania even after the communists had assumed full power in Roumania), and in his reference to Russian rights before the Russo-Japanese War of 1904, as a justification for acquiring the Liaotung Peninsula and the two great Manchurian railways in his 1945 treaty with the (Nationalist) Government of China.

*   *   *

The policy of forced industrialisation, financed by a low standard of living for workers and peasants, was pursued in Eastern Europe for several months after Stalin's death. A new measure in the same direction was a 'currency reform' introduced in Czechoslovakia in May 1953, which was designed to confiscate the savings of the skilled workers and lower the purchasing power of the whole people. Rage at this new blow, combined with a certain boldness, perhaps caused by the almost simultaneous death of Stalin and of the 'little Stalin' of Czechoslovakia, Klement Gottwald, produced a short but violent explosion in the Czech industrial city of Plzen, where crowds of workers for some hours took over the whole city, seized public buildings and put forward demands not only for better material conditions but for political liberty. Two weeks later came the great rising of 17 June 1953 in East Berlin, which grew into a massive insurrection of the working class of the whole of Eastern Germany, and clearly expressed the demand not only for economic betterment but also for democratic government and for the unity of Germany. The insurrection was suppressed by the Soviet army. The complete failure of the East German security police to control the crowds was probably one of the immediate causes of the downfall in Moscow of the security chief of the whole Soviet empire, Lavrenti Beria. This in turn led to a reduction in the powers of the Soviet security police and to recommendations from Moscow to the East European communist leaders to use milder methods towards their subjects. There now began a 'New Course' in some of the satellites.

The first and most striking changes came in Hungary. The 'little Stalin', Mátyás Rákosi, was obliged to give up the Premiership, though he retained his office of first secretary of the communist party. His successor as Premier, Imre Nagy, introduced a programme of reforms. Collectivisation of agriculture was halted, peasants were permitted to leave existing collectives, and even to dissolve collectives if a majority of members should wish this. As a result, in the next year a third of the members of collectives seceded, and 10% of all collectives were dissolved. The pace of industrialisation was reduced, and greater priority was given to consumers' goods output. Thousands of political prisoners were released, and persons deported from their homes were allowed to return. In Czechoslovakia there was no noticeable relaxation of political terror, but the same economic concessions were granted as in Hungary, and were more effectively carried out. The result was a steadily rising standard of living for the Czech and Slovak peoples, whose material conditions at the end of the 1950's were comparable with those of Western Europe. In Roumania there were fewer economic concessions, much less efficiently carried out. In Poland there was little economic improvement, but a more critical attitude was permitted in the press and publications. Only in Bulgaria did the political terror and the economic pressure remain virtually unchanged.

* * *

In the spring of 1955 the fall in Moscow of G. M. Malenkov, who had been associated with increased output of consumers' goods, gave Rákosi the chance to remove Nagy and place one of his own creatures in the Premiership. But he was unable to return to the methods of the Stalin era. The new leader of the Soviet party, N. S. Khrushchov, was determined to rectify Stalin's error of antagonising Yugoslavia. If he was to be reconciled with President Tito, he would have to make the satellite leaders, who had persecuted the real or alleged friends of Tito in their countries, drastically change their policies. Khrushchov insisted on the maintenance of the concessions of the 'New Course' period. At the 20th Congress of the CPSU, held in February 1956, he made his famous speech in secret session, in which he denounced the crimes and follies of Stalin. Knowledge of the speech spread rapidly through the communist parties of Eastern Europe, and in the summer of 1956 (after a version of the text had been published by the United States government) it became known to the people outside the party ranks.

Immediately after the 20th Congress the 'little Stalin' of Poland, Boleslaw Bierut, died. In the spring several leading Polish followers of Stalin were removed from their posts. In May the university students of Prague and Bratislava put forward a series of demands, not only for improvements in their material and professional conditions, but also for greater political freedom. Though the demands were refused, they created a stir. In June the workers of Poznan followed the example of Plzen and Berlin, took over the whole city and put forward economic and political demands. The Polish army put down the insurrection with little bloodshed, and the Polish government publicly admitted that its mistaken policies were responsible for the workers' discontent, rejecting by implication the opinion simultaneously expressed in the Soviet Union that it had been caused by foreign 'imperialist' intervention. During June several stormy meetings were held in Budapest by an intellectual discussion group known as the Petöffi Club. The violent attacks which the Club made on the Rákosi regime were followed not by the arrest of the critics but by the removal of Rákosi from the first secretaryship of the party, which took place on 18 July 1956. His successor, however, was his former most intimate collaborator, associated with all his most brutal policies, Ernö Gerö.

During the summer of 1956 Eastern Europe was demonstrably in ferment. The longing both for political freedom and for independence from the Soviet Union was making itself felt even in the communist parties, above all in Poland and Hungary, but to some extent also in Czechoslovakia and Roumania, a little even in the still more ruthlessly repressed Bulgaria. The attitude of the Soviet leaders vacillated. Khrushchov seems to have aimed at reconciliation with Yugoslavia and at creating a state of affairs in the satellites in which the communist parties by milder policies could win genuine popularity, and in which the Soviet Union, by relaxing its grip on the satellites, could win the friendship of their peoples. At the same time, however, he was alarmed by the Poznan insurrection and by the possible consequences of Yugoslav influence in Eastern Europe.

The crisis came in October 1956. The Central Committee of the Polish communist party decided not to re-elect the Soviet Marshal Rokossovski to its Politburo, and to entrust the post of first secretary of the party to Wladyslaw Gomulka, the 'nationalist deviationist' disgraced in 1948, who had been released from prison in 1955. There was a strong movement within the party, especially in the capital, Warsaw, and among the younger generation, for far-reaching democratic reforms. This movement swept Gomulka into power. The existing first secretary, Eduard Ochab, decided to swim with the tide, and the majority of his colleagues followed him. While the fateful meeting of the Central Committee of the Polish party was in session, Khrushchov, accompanied by other Soviet leaders, arrived in Warsaw. For a time it looked as if there would be war between the Soviet forces in Poland and the Polish army and security police (which were loyal to Gomulka and Ochab). But Khrushchov decided to accept Gomulka and to agree to the reforms which his advent was bound to bring, and disaster was averted.

A similar crisis occurred a few days later in Hungary. But Gerö lacked the patriotism and common-sense of Ochab. He refused concessions, and gave orders to fire on the demonstrators. Imre Nagy was nominally appointed Prime Minister, but had at first no real power, and Soviet forces (whether invited by Gerö or acting on independent orders from Moscow is not certain) were soon involved in fighting against Hungarian armed workers and students, and some units of the Hungarian army. The first stage of this Hungarian-Soviet war ended in a Hungarian victory. An armistice was signed, Nagy assumed real power, and formed a government in which the socialist and peasant parties were represented, with a programme of genuine democratic liberties and of neutrality in international policy. But Hungary's freedom lasted only a week. On 4th November 1956 the Soviet forces, which had been reinforced for several days beforehand, launched a general attack. Budapest was captured, the last strongholds of the armed workers in their fortresses of Csepel and Dunapentele were stormed, the leaders of the workers' councils were executed, and a puppet government was set up under János Kádár, a communist who had served in Nagy's government and betrayed him. Nagy himself was captured by fraud, held in prison for nearly two years and then executed. No one knows to what physical or mental tortures this Hungarian patriot and veteran communist was subjected, but it is certain that he made no confession, and betrayed neither his friends nor his country.

* * *

The events in Poland and Hungary showed two very

important things. The first is that the working class utterly rejected the communist leaders and policies of 1945–1956 and demanded national independence. The regimes claimed to rule in the name of the workers, but the workers saw in them instruments of Soviet colonial rule and totalitarian tyranny. The second is that the intellectual youth was united against the regimes. This is the more remarkable when it is remembered that the students of 1956 consisted predominantly of children of workers and poor peasants who could not have got a higher education under the pre-war regimes. One of the positive achievements of the regimes had been that they had thrown open the secondary schools and colleges to the youth of the poorer classes. These young men owed everything to the regime. The communist leaders had hoped that they would thus create a new 'toilers' intelligentsia' which would provide the brains of the totalitarian regime and the ruling cadres of the Soviet colonial system. But the young workers and peasants had not only learned facts and skills, they had learned ideas and they had learned to think. They had seen through the hypocrisies and deceits of the communists, and they had become more aware than ever of the sufferings of their people. In this they had in fact followed the example of their predecessors of the 'bourgeois intelligentsia' who had led the democratic movement against the pre-war Polish and Hungarian dictatorships. In 1956 it was the Polish and Hungarian educated youth which led the revolutionary movement. This was a terrible lesson for the communists not only in Poland and Hungary but in the Soviet Union itself.

* * *

During 1957 Poland enjoyed a great deal of liberty. At first there were even public discussions, at meetings and in print, of the fundamental principles of Marxism. 'Revisionists' questioned the dogmas of Lenin and Stalin from a Marxist point of view, and others even criticised Marx. By the summer public discussion of this sort had been stopped, but private conversations were possible, without fear of police informers or repression, as late as 1960. Workers' councils were organised in the factories, but they were gradually shorn of their powers, and by 1958 had ceased to play a role of any importance. The Catholic Church was freed from almost all government interference, and religious instruction was reintroduced into the schools. But from 1959 onwards the communist party began a counter-offensive, and by 1961 religious teaching had been ended in a majority of the schools. Nevertheless in 1961 the church was still freer than it had been in Poland since 1939, and much freer than in any other East European country. The peasants perhaps made the greatest gains from the events of October 1956. Collective farms almost ceased to exist, and farmers received much better prices for their produce. By 1960 there were signs that the government was planning some steps in the direction of collectivisation, but it looked as if the methods would be mild and the pace slow. The improved conditions granted by Khrushchov to the peasants in the Soviet Union made it unlikely that brutal pressure would be exercised in Poland. Nevertheless there is no doubt that the Poles' hopes of 1956 were progressively disappointed during the 1960's. This was not, however, primarily a result of Soviet intervention. Gomulka himself had always been a fanatical communist. He had never shared the belief in political liberty of those who had swept him back to power. He believed in one-party dictatorship by communists. He also believed in unreservedly supporting Soviet foreign policy. He did, however, object to the use of total police terror and to Soviet intervention in internal Polish administration.

* * *

In Hungary reconquest was followed by reprisals, including some executions and many prison sentences. In 1958 a campaign of rapid collectivisation of agriculture was pushed through. Complete devotion to the Soviet Union was loudly proclaimed. However, in the course of the next years the new leader Kádár showed himself, by communist standards, a relatively liberal and open-minded person. At the end of the 1960's Hungary had the most flexible and intelligent economic policy of all communist countries, had attained a higher standard of living than any except Eastern Germany, and allowed a wider measure of personal and intellectual freedom (outside the purely political sphere in which of course no argument was permitted). To this extent it may be said that the heroic effort of the Revolution of 1956 did not go unrewarded.

The situation of all the East European communist regimes was affected by the Soviet-Chinese quarrel of the 1960's. The Soviet leaders were no longer in a position to give direct orders. They needed the support of the East European parties in their quarrel with the Chinese, and for this they had to pay the price of greater internal sovereignty. The East European leaders had more freedom of political manœuvre.

The only state which took the Chinese side was Albania. This extremely backward country, with a predominantly Moslem peasant population, has been ruled since 1945 by a handful of communists led by Enver Hoxha, its 'little Stalin'. His success has been due partly to ruthless terror and partly to able exploitation of the national hostility to Yugoslavia. A third of the Albanians in the world live in Yugoslavia, and the desire to include them in a single Albanian fatherland is certainly strong. The breach between Moscow and Belgrade in 1948 was a blessing to Hoxha. It enabled him to rid himself of his main rival, Kochi Dzodze, as an 'agent of Tito', and to denounce any suggestions of more liberal policies as Titoism. Khrushchov's policy of conciliation distressed him. There was never a 'New Course' in Albania: Stalinist methods were not abandoned. It was perfectly consistent with Hoxha's past record that, when opposition to Khrushchov's 'peaceful coexistence' policy was led by the Chinese communists, he should have taken the Chinese side. The very isolation of Albania, which has no common frontier with the Soviet Union or with any satellite, though a potential source of danger to the Albanian communist regime, was also a source of strength. Soviet economic aid had to be sacrificed, as Albania in the 1960's became the main mouthpiece of Chinese attacks on Soviet policy, and eventually Soviet-Albanian relations were formally broken. Chinese material aid probably did not adequately replace Soviet aid, but the primitive economy was kept going, and material progress was achieved. At the end of the 1960's Albania even began to pursue reconciliation with Yugoslavia, and the Belgrade government for its part made serious efforts to improve the conditions of the 1,000,000 Albanians in Kosovo and Macedonia, and to allow them to use the Albanian flag and to take pride in their Albanian national culture. The Albanian government also began to take the first halting steps towards re-establishing cultural relations with non-communist countries in Europe.

The opportunities offered by the Soviet-Chinese conflict were used with greater discretion (due to less favourable geographical circumstances) but with considerable skill by the Roumanian leaders. The crisis in Soviet-Roumanian relations came early in 1962. The Soviet government wished to use the Council of Mutual Economic Aid (*Comecon*), to which all the European communist governments belonged, to introduce a greater measure of co-ordination between the economies, encouraging each to specialise in the fields in which it had the best exploitable resources, the whole area of course to produce the optimum results in the interests of the Soviet overlord. From the Roumanian point of view this plan, whatever its theoretical merits, was objectionable because it would perpetuate the difference between the more and the less industrialised states. Roumania, which was relatively less advanced, had made rapid progress in industry in the preceding years, and was determined not to arrest this advance. The Roumanian government therefore refused to accept the new plan, and insisted on the right of each individual member country to determine its own economic policy. Faced with this strong criticism, Khrushchov gave up his plan.

Having obtained effective recognition of its right to

economic independence, the Roumanian government proceeded to take a more independent line in a wider field. Cultural relations with the rest of Europe were rapidly developed. Nothing had caused greater rage in Roumania in preceding years—both within and outside the communist party—than the attempt of the Soviet leaders to Russify the Roumanians, by interfering with their language and distorting their history to show that Slav influences had been more important in Roumanian culture than Latin influences, and by severing Roumania's cultural relations with France and Italy. Now the Roumanian leaders reasserted the Latin nature of Roumanian culture, renewed their contacts with France and Italy, and extended them to Britain, Germany and the smaller Western countries. Trade with countries outside the Soviet camp also grew rapidly. Roumania was the first of the East European communist states to establish full diplomatic relations with the German Federal Republic. In the Soviet-Chinese dispute the Roumanian communists occupied a middle position. At the United Nations, the Roumanian representative at times took an attitude different from, though never directly opposed to, that of the Soviet government. In the Israeli-Arab war of 1967 Roumania took a neutral position, and throughout the late 1960's Roumania's relations with Israel remained good. At the same time Roumanian leaders spoke with self-restraint of the Soviet Union, and never allowed any provocative behaviour by Roumanian citizens. Internally, the communist party's control was undiminished, but its rule was exercised in a markedly more humane manner: as in Hungary, outside the purely political sphere, considerable personal and intellectual freedom was permitted.

In the late 1960's pressures for reform were at last felt in Czechoslovakia. The first sign was more active opposition by the Slovak communists to the excessive centralism of the Prague government. Then Czech intellectuals began to express heretical opinions about liberty of thought: the Writers' Union became a centre of dissent. Meanwhile economic conditions notably deteriorated, and the harmful consequences of doctrinaire and bureaucratic central planning could no longer be denied. Economic reforms were accepted in principle, but not implemented in practice. The reformers began to argue that economic reform could not get going without some political reform. All these pressures combined in the winter of 1967–1968 in a demand within the party for the replacement of the party boss, Antonín Novotný. In January 1968 he was replaced by a comparatively unknown Slovak communist, Alexander Dubček. In the next months there was a remarkable upsurge of democratic opinion, in which the intellectuals took the lead but the workers soon joined with enthusiasm. Censorship was abolished, the truth about the Gottwald period was published and the official falsifications of earlier Czech and Slovak history were repudiated. Preparations were made for a new Congress of the Communist Party, at which it was clear that the bosses of the 1960's would be swept away and their places taken by new men of democratic outlook but unknown intentions. At the same time Dubček and his colleagues, while permitting and largely approving of these developments, repeatedly asserted that the communist party would maintain its monopoly of political power, and that Czechoslovakia would remain loyal to its alliance with the Soviet Union.

If the Soviet leaders had been primarily concerned with the interests of socialism, then it may be argued that they would have allowed events to take their course, trusting to the traditional belief of the Czechs and Slovaks that Russia was their best friend. This was what idealistically minded communists and socialists in Czechoslovakia and in the rest of Europe hoped that they would do. But the truth was that the Soviet leaders' first priority was something else: the preservation of an empire. They feared that the Czechoslovak party would not long remain in control: they noted with horror that non-communist political organisations were being founded with official permission. They feared that if real power slipped out of communist hands, the government, even if nominally led by communists, would no longer maintain the alliance with the Soviet Union: voices were already being raised (though admittedly only by individuals with no organised following) in favour of neutrality. They feared the consequences of the example of Czechoslovakia in neighbouring countries, and in this they were strongly supported by the frightened rulers of Poland and of East Germany. During the spring and early summer their diplomats and their press took an increasingly angry tone. This posture was self-defeating: the more attacks came from Moscow, the more nationalist the Czechs and Slovaks became, and the more difficult it was for Dubček and his team to persuade them to restrain themselves. In July 1968 the Politburos of the Soviet and Czechoslovak parties met at Černa-nad-Tisou in eastern Slovakia, and some days later the leaders of the Polish, East German, Hungarian, Bulgarian and Soviet parties came to Bratislava. These confrontations were unpleasant, but it appeared that an agreement had been reached. However, whether because the Soviet leaders convinced themselves that Dubček had not kept his promises, or because they had themselves not intended to keep their own word, or for some other reason still unknown, Brezhnev decided to invade Czechoslovakia. Military preparations had been made long beforehand, and on 21 August a large invasion force, which included a few Polish, East German, Bulgarian and Hungarian troops, occupied the country within a few hours. The Dubček government decided not to order armed resistance, but there was impressive and widespread popular passive resistance, in which the Czechoslovak army co-operated, especially by the provision of broadcasting facilities. The Soviet leaders were sufficiently impressed by this, and sufficiently unwilling to risk large-scale bloodshed, for it to seem preferable to release Dubček and his close colleagues, whom they had abducted and brutally treated, and allow them to resume the government. It took the Soviet government nearly two years of pressure and intrigue to split the leadership, eliminate the most active people, drive thousands of Czechs into exile, dismiss some hundreds from their jobs and threaten larger numbers into silent conformity. By the summer of 1970 censorship had been thoroughly reimposed, history was being refalsified, the press was obediently regurgitating the well-tried lies of the old days, and abject flattery of the big bosses in Moscow filled the air.

The invasion of Czechoslovakia was made the occasion for a new formulation of an old doctrine. Stalin had claimed that the first duty of all communists everywhere must always be to protect the Soviet Union. Brezhnev declared that whenever 'socialism' was in danger, all 'socialist states' must join in helping the threatened 'socialist' government, whether or not it had asked for help. This meant of course that the Soviet government—which was the sole judge of whether a threat existed—could at any time order its army and those of the East European states to invade the territory of any communist-ruled country whose policies displeased it. The word 'socialist' was of course ambiguous: it was not clear whether it applied to Yugoslavia, or could be extended to other countries in Europe or outside. It certainly covered Roumania, and for some months that country appeared to be in danger. However, the tough attitude of its leaders, who, without provoking the Soviet Union in any way, made it clear that they would resist invasion and thus force the Soviet army to shed blood, had the desired effect. It was probably helped by a warning statement by President Johnson, and by the visit of President Nixon to Roumania a year later.

The truth was that in 1970 there was in Central Europe a Soviet Empire. This Empire was bitterly hated by all the subject peoples, including most members of communist parties as well as those outside the parties. The last nation which still had affection for the Russians, the Czechs, were turned by the 1968 invasion into enemies. At any time since 1945, if the Soviet leaders had been content with a mere dominant position in Eastern Europe, such as imperial powers had held in the past, they could have had it with the consent not only of the Western Powers but of the Central European peoples. But this traditional imperial status was not enough for the Soviet leaders. They insisted on going further: they must oppress, exploit and nationally humiliate the peoples of these lands. They must go further still: they must falsify their history, deprive them of their culture and destroy their nationality. The Soviet policy had all the unpleasant features of old-style imperialism, but it was much worse. It was worse even than Ottoman Turkish rule in its militant days: the Turks had treated non-Moslems as second-class citizens, but they had not tried to deprive them of their identity. The Soviet Empire in 1970 was the most oppressive empire that had ever existed in the heart of Europe; its rule was hated and rejected by the Central Europeans; and for this reason Central Europe was one of the most explosive and dangerous areas in the world.

6

Communism
and the New Nations

THE aims of communism are not confined to Russia, China
and Eastern Europe. The Soviet leaders remain convinced
that the scientific laws of Marxism-Leninism are applicable
to the human race, and it remains the duty of communists
not to sit back and let history do their job for them but
to put every possible effort into the acceleration of its ineluctable processes. It is no longer maintained that all
human societies need pass through capitalism. It is possible
to leap straight from 'feudalism' (by which communists in
practice mean little more than a pre-industrial economy
with a more or less clearly defined agrarian ruling class) to
'socialism'. Mongolia is quoted as the first example. But
whether a given society need pass through capitalism or not,
it must in the end reach the stage of 'socialism' and it can
enter this stage only by revolution. Socialist revolutions can
be carried out only by Marxist-Leninist parties, recognised
as such by the international communist movement, and
they can result only in the establishment of a one-party
regime controlled by such a party, denying all liberty to
persons and groups of other views. The Soviet social-politi-
cal blueprint, as it was worked out in the 1930's, remains,
with minor variations, binding on all nations.

This was stated in clear and categorical terms in the
Moscow Declaration of the twelve ruling communist parties
in November 1957. This stated that, though the path to
socialism may vary according to particular circumstances,
there are certain 'basic laws applicable in all countries em-
barking on a socialist course'. First of these laws is 'guidance

of the working masses by the working class, the core of which is the Marxist-Leninist party, in effecting a proletarian revolution in one form or another and establishing one form or another of the dictatorship of the proletariat'.

The practical limits to the principle that there are different roads to socialism were shown by the suppression of the Hungarian Revolution in 1956, and by the destruction of the Hungarian workers' councils, which more genuinely represented the working class than any organisation since the free Russian soviets of early 1917.

In recent years communists have distinguished between 'peaceful revolution' (or 'the parliamentary road to socialism') and 'violent revolution'. As examples of the first type, Mikoyan, in his speech to the Twentieth Congress of the CPSU in February 1956, quoted post-war Czechoslovakia and Eastern Germany. It is perfectly clear from the large communist literature on the subject that a 'peaceful revolution' means the surrender of the opponents of the communists without a fight. In this case the communists get power without having to use force, and then use their power forcibly to destroy their surrendered opponents. Revolution is 'violent' when the opponents resist, and a civil war is needed to get the communists into power. In other words, the difference between 'violent' and 'peaceful' revolution is that in the former case violence is used before and after seizure of power, and in the latter case only after.

* * *

In the field of international relations a similar distinction exists between the triumph of 'socialism' by war or by peaceful means. Triumph by peaceful means is possible if 'the capitalists' (that is, all governments independent of the Sino-Soviet bloc) will surrender piecemeal to the demands of 'the socialist camp' without resistance. This is what the Soviet leaders mean by 'peaceful co-existence'. Major wars are to be avoided, and in the meantime 'economic means' are to be used to bring about the destruction of 'the imperialists'— that is, the ultimate imposition of communist party rule on the peoples of all countries, not only of under-developed societies but also of the advanced industrial societies of the West. The 'economic means' include not only competition in trade and aid but also all available forms of propaganda, subversion and revolutionary activity.

The declaration signed in Moscow in December 1960 by the representatives of 81 communist parties endorsed this doctrine. It stressed the growing strength of 'the socialist camp' (the Sino-Soviet bloc), which would soon far exceed the strength of the 'imperialists'. In the words of this statement: 'In the conditions of peaceful co-existence, favourable opportunities are created for developing the class struggle in capitalist countries and the national liberation movement of peoples of colonial and dependent countries . . . Peaceful co-existence of states with different social systems does not mean a reconciliation between the socialist and bourgeois ideologies . . . The co-existence of states with different social systems is a form of class struggle between socialism and capitalism.'

The Moscow declaration of 1960 bears the signature of the Chinese Communist Party. In the preceding months a fierce argument had developed between the Soviet and Chinese parties, on the subject of whether war was necessary for the victory of 'socialism'. The story of this argument cannot be told here. Neither Soviet nor Chinese communists completely ruled out the possibility either of war or of victory without war. But whereas the Chinese insisted that it was virtually certain that 'the imperialists' would fight, and a world war be necessary, the Soviet leaders maintained that victory without war was probable. There was and is, however, no difference between them as to the aim, which was and is the imposition on one country after another, by appropriate means and stages, of communist party dictatorship.

*　　*　　*

Communists of course deny that their efforts to accelerate the ineluctable progress of the peoples of the under-developed societies towards 'socialism' are imperialistic. On the contrary, they claim that they have a proud record of struggle against imperialism. Already in the 1920's they gave what support they could to Asian and African nationalist movements directed against the colonial and imperialist Great Powers. They supported Kemal Atatürk in Turkey, they showed sympathy to Reza Khan in Persia, King Amanulla in Afghanistan and the early Wafd movement in Egypt. They urged the French communists to help the revolt of the Moroccan insurgents of the Riff under Abd el-Krim, and the Vietnamese nationalists in Indo-China. Most important of all, they organised the alliance between the Kuomintang and the communists in China from 1923 to 1927.

Yet even in the 1920's the contradiction between the aims of Asian nationalists and communists could not be resolved. The Soviet leaders were more interested in the communists than in the nationalists, but they were more interested in Soviet imperial interests than in either of them. The most daring theorist of the alliance with Asian nationalism, the Tatar communist Mirza Sultan-Galiev, was disgraced in 1923. The alliance with nationalism was maintained longest, and ended most tragically, in China, where Chiang Kai-shek massacred the workers of Shanghai and made common cause with northern warlords.

The rise of Hitler and the growing threat from Japan made Stalin and his colleagues think less than ever of the encouragement of Asian or African nationalism against the colonial Powers. During the Soviet-German war of 1941–1945 communists in Asia were urged to support the war effort, which in their countries often meant to support the British war effort. The Indian communists made themselves hated by Indian nationalists by their devotion to the allied cause. In Burma the communists played their part in bringing the nationalists, and their Burma National Army, over from the Japanese to the allied side. In the Philippines and Malaya the communists played a leading part in the resistance to the Japanese occupation.

After the war, however, communist policy rapidly reverted

to militant hositility. There was no longer a fascist danger, and the struggle against 'the capitalists' could be resumed with renewed energy. Everywhere the communists of Asia did their best to outbid the non-communist nationalist movements in the struggle against the colonial Powers.

A new problem, however, arose when the British government accepted the independence of India, Pakistan, Burma and Ceylon, the United States government carried out its previous promise to give independence to the Philippines, and after a period of bitter fighting and of pressure at the United Nations the Dutch recognised Indonesian independence. What should be the attitude of the Soviet government, and of the local communist parties, to these new independent governments?

The answer was at first repudiation. The Soviet government established diplomatic relations with the new states, but Soviet spokesmen made it perfectly clear that they regarded their independence as fictitious. Nehru, Nu and Soekarno were puppets of 'the imperialists'. The British empire was being maintained in India by other means. In Indonesia admittedly the Dutch had lost most of their power, but they had merely been replaced by American imperialists. In 1948 India was not independent but Roumania was fully independent. This assertion can at once be seen for a true statement of fact, as soon as one understands what 'independence' meant to Stalin. Roumania was indeed completely independent of any influence other than that of the Soviet Union, while India was open to various influences from many sides. In the last years of Stalin true 'independence' could only mean complete subjection to his will. This was not of course stated in such crude terms. The most usual formulation was that the Asian peoples could obtain independence only under the 'hegemony of the working class', by which was of course meant under the dictatorship of the communist party. Asian communist parties were advised to revolt against the new governments. In 1948 there were communist insurrections in the Telengana district in India, in Burma, in the Philippines and in Indonesia. In Malaya, which was still a British colony, a communist rebellion also broke out in 1948.

In Indo-China war against the French, under communist leadership, began in 1946. This situation was, however, a different one, for the communist-led resistance movement against the Japanese had not been disarmed, and the French government would not agree to terms for Indo-Chinese independence acceptable to the nationalists. For this reason the Vietnamese war against the French proved much stronger than the other communist rebellions, and in fact achieved partial victory with the partition of Indo-China in 1954.

Of the other rebellions, the Indian was suppressed by the Indian army, but the others dragged on, at considerable cost to the governments and at still greater cost to the peoples, for a number of years, without, however, at any time coming within sight of victory.

* * *

Meanwhile the Chinese communists had won power in their own civil war in 1949. Though it is probable that even then there was distrust in Moscow of Chinese pretensions, official Soviet spokesmen praised the Chinese achievement, and emphasised that in China victory had been achieved under 'the hegemony of the working class'.

It was from China, not from Russia, that the initiative came for the reversal of policy towards the new states. The Korean War showed clearly that India was in fact no satellite of the West, that Indian foreign policy was made only in New Delhi. The Chinese established comparatively friendly relations with India by 1951. During the next years Chinese diplomacy sought to make friends in southern Asia. In April 1955 Chou En-lai did his best to charm the representatives of Asian and African nations at the Bandung conference. By now Stalin had been dead two years, and the first rounds of the struggle for the succession were over—Beria arrested in June 1953 and Malenkov dismissed in February 1955. The victor, N. S. Khrushchov, could turn from the fight against his colleagues, and pay attention to world politics. In the autumn of 1955 the arms deal was made with Egypt, using Czechoslovakia as the instrument, and Khrushchov and Bulganin made their spectacular tour of India and Burma. For the next years the main emphasis of Soviet foreign policy, and the main direction of Soviet expansion, were towards the underdeveloped societies.

These, from the Soviet point of view, were divided into three groups.

First were the states which were both independent and neutral in foreign policy. These, in Soviet terminology, were politically independent but not economically independent. They could become economically independent only when they had freed themselves from all ties of dependence on the West, and had made full use of 'the unselfish aid of the socialist camp'. This was a much more realistic and tactful formulation than that of the Stalin era, but it was not by any means clear how great the difference of substance was. It was not clear how far this double process had to go before 'economic independence' could be recognised.

This category of the 'politically independent' states which have yet to win their 'economic independence' certainly included in 1960 India, Burma, Indonesia, the United Arab Republic and Iraq. It probably included such Latin American states as Mexico and Argentina. Such small African states as Ghana, Mali, Morocco and Ethiopia presumably also belonged to this category.

The second main category consisted of those states which were independent but associated with the West. These were recognised as neither politically nor economically independent. 'The imperialists' were ruling and exploiting them, though by indirect means. This group in 1960 included Turkey, Persia, Pakistan, Siam and the Philippines as well as most of the smaller Latin American republics.

It should be noted that the distinction between the first and second categories is one of foreign policy. Any member of the second group would immediately count as a member of the first group as soon as it abandoned its alliance or

107

co-operation with the United States. 'Political independence' simply means absence of close relations with the United States, while 'economic independence' means dependence for trade and loans on the Soviet bloc.

The third category consisted of the few residual colonial territories ruled by Britain or France; the still substantial Portuguese colonial empire; Southern Rhodesia and South Africa. The last two were of course in 1970 not subject to any metropolitan government, but the majority of their populations consisted of black Africans (of various languages and customs) ruled by white African minorities of European origin.

The objectives of Soviet and communist policy are distinct in each of these three cases. In colonies the aim is to stimulate and exploit nationalist movements. In independent allied states it is to stimulate movements for neutralism. In independent and neutralist states it is to transform neutralism into 'neutralism against the West', and this in turn into membership of the Soviet bloc. Each of these three policies can be considered in turn.

* * *

Communist influence on nationalist movements has been small in the colonial period, whether in Asia between the world wars or in Africa after the Second World War. However, the Soviet leaders have shown a good understanding of the problems of leadership in such movements. The history of the Russian revolutionary movement, from the 1860's to 1917, has taught them the importance of the small modern-educated intellectual elite—the *intelligentsia*, to use a word first invented in Russia a century ago to describe a social group which first appeared in Russia. They understand (as many politicians, journalists and civil servants of colonial and ex-colonial Powers still have not understood) that it is from this social group that the leaders of the new nations are formed. Between the world wars the communists made efforts to attract members of the Asian *intelligentsia* studying in Europe. Their most conspicuous success was Ho Chi-Minh. With Nehru and Soe-karno they were less fortunate. Nkrumah and Kenyatta were both influenced by Marxism, but apparently not very profoundly.

During the 1950's much greater efforts have been made. Africans have been trained, both in the sciences and in techniques of propaganda and subversion, in Prague, Moscow and other centres in the Soviet bloc. The results are most uncertain. There have been many disappointments. Some Africans bitterly resented the restrictions placed on freedom of speech and movement. Some even came up against an arrogance which seemed to them indistinguish-able from the colour bars and racial discrimination so often encountered in European and American cities. Others were favourably impressed by Soviet or East European regimes. Others again were recruited to communism not in countries of the Soviet bloc but in the West, especially in Paris and London. It is quite impossible to estimate the degree of success of the Soviet leaders, either in implanting pro-Soviet sympathies into Africans who have come to Europe—West or East—for serious studies, or in training smaller numbers of full-time subversive agents.

* * *

Another extremely important field for Soviet activity, designed to influence colonial situations, has been the United Nations. Here it is not difficult to see the Soviet strategy. It was of course already obvious in 1960 that Afri-can nationalism was a strong and growing force. Almost every responsible political leader except Dr. Salazar and Dr. Verwoerd admitted this. But two things for some years remained uncertain—the pace of the movement towards African independence, and the circumstances in which it would be won. The Soviet aim was to ensure that the pace was recklessly fast, and that the parting between the African peoples and their colonial rulers took place in an atmo-sphere of maximum hatred and violence. The greater the anarchy and bloodshed, the better for the Soviet cause. If possible, not only soldiers and bureaucrats but all private citizens of the formerly ruling nation had to be expelled. The new states could not remain in anarchy for ever. They could not survive without advisers and experts from advanced nations. But if they should quarrel irreparably, not only with their former masters but with all nations which maintained friendly relations with their former masters, then they could get advisers and experts only from the Soviet bloc. Engineers, scientists and administrators would be offered in generous quantities from the Soviet Union, Eastern Germany, Czechoslovakia, China or other bloc countries. Once installed, they would wield the decisive power, and they would train their pupils not only in science and engineering but also in the arts of security police terror, guerrilla warfare and subversion against neighbouring countries. Soon 'popular democracies' could be created in Africa. The ineluctable progress from tribalism to 'socialism' would be brilliantly accelerated, bypassing both 'feudalism' and 'capitalism'. A new Soviet colonial empire would have been founded.

The tragedy of the Congo showed considerable progress in this direction by the beginning of 1961. It is true that the United Nations did not accept the more extravagant claims made by the Soviet spokesmen. But some principles became generally accepted which were of undoubted benefit to the Soviet cause, and were accepted largely because the Soviet attitude had been so uncompromising. One was that only black African states can be regarded as impartial in African affairs, white Africans being considered prejudiced by definition. Another was that the only European countries entitled to send troops to the United Nations forces in the Congo are the traditional neutrals, such as Ireland or Sweden. Ghana and Guinea, committed to the Lumumba side in the conflict, were nevertheless considered impartial, while the European nations which belonged to NATO, an alliance whose field of operation is confined to Europe, and of which Belgium is a member, were excluded as incapable of taking a fair attitude. Another success was the general acceptance of the view that any action undertaken by the Belgian government in defence of its citizens was 'imperialistic', and that all Belgian citizens in the Congo were guilty of some sort of political original sin. It had been the original intention that independent Congo should allow Belgians to live and work there, and that Belgian business should continue, just as British business continued in India. But by the end of 1960 the Soviet view, that as long as a single business-man of the formerly ruling nation does business in a country, that country is not yet 'independent', had become tacitly accepted. It is hardly an exaggeration to say that 'world opinion', as accepted in the corridors of the United Nations, had come to regard Belgian citizens in the Congo very much as 'public opinion' in the Third Reich regarded Jews in Germany—as some sort of vermin. And because Mr. Tshombe in Katanga was on good terms with Belgians, he was viewed, by African nationalists and their European sympathisers, very much as a 'nigger-lover' was regarded in Alabama.

The acceptance of such opinions must be regarded as a success for Soviet foreign policy. On the other hand there were still African governments which did not subscribe to these views.

* * *

An important aspect of Soviet and communist thinking about colonial and newly independent tropical Africa is their doctrine about the formation of nationality in these countries. The chief Soviet expert on this subject, the late Professor I. I. Potekhin, developed a theory on the development of 'tribes' into 'peoples', and of 'peoples' into 'bourgeois nations'. This theory did not formally conflict with the familiar Marxist stages of development from patriarchal to feudal, and from feudal to capitalist relationships, but in practice it largely superseded it. He laid great stress on the formation, from the large number of dialects and minor languages, of a small number of standardised literary languages. It is clear that Potekhin considered the development of languages as no less important a means of creating national consciousness than the development of capitalism. The long experience of the Soviet communists in the manipulation of dialects and languages, and of the policy of 'divide and rule' (especially in the Volga valley and Turkestan) made them well qualified to handle linguistic nationalism. The arbitrary nature of the frontiers drawn between European colonies also provided them with excellent opportunities. The Somalis, the Ewe and the Bakongo are examples of language-groups divided between two or more African states. Potekhin even envisaged the creation of an artificial single language, and consequent single national consciousness, among the Nilotic peoples, at present divided between Sudan, Congo, Uganda and Kenya. The Nilotic languages, he argued, possess 'a single basic vocabulary', and three of them have an identical grammatical structure. 'It is by no means out of the question that in favourable conditions the Nilotics may be able to form themselves into a single people.' In the Congo crisis of 1960–1961 the Soviet government upheld the 'centralising' as opposed to the 'federal' tendency. But should the greater part of the Congo elude Soviet influence, it might be possible to use a small portion, controlled by pro-Soviet forces, as a base from which to agitate for a future Nilotic state.

* * *

In independent states allied to the West, Soviet propaganda stresses the alliance between the United States, the local plutocracy and local dictatorships. Those local business-men who have important business relations with Americans or West Europeans are branded as 'compradores' and reactionaries, while those whose enterprises compete with Western business interests are praised as 'national bourgeois'. The criterion is one of foreign policy, and other possible distinctions between local business-men (those who are rich and those who are poor, those who treat their workers better and those who treat them worse) are ignored. The existence of dictatorships is arbitrarily attributed to American policy. If, however, the American government shows hostility to a dictatorship, this is 'imperialist intervention'. For example, the cruelties of General Perez Jimenez in Venezuela were blamed on the United States, but when the American Ambassador in Buenos Aires in 1945 tried to put pressure on the dictator Juan Peron, this was Yankee interference in Argentine affairs. When Perez was overthrown, the communists were at first pleased. But when the Democratic Action leader, Romulo Betancourt, became President, and pursued a policy of friendship with the United States, while introducing a genuinely democratic regime, he was denounced by Moscow as a Yankee puppet.

The case of Iran is of some interest. In 1945 the Soviet government (whose forces had been in Iran, by agreement with its British and American allies, since 1941) set up a communist regime in Azerbaidjan, the north-western province which borders with the Azerbaidjan SSR of the Soviet Union, and also supported a Kurdish autonomous authority in Mahabad. A year later Soviet troops were withdrawn, and both regimes collapsed, leaving a bitter memory of Soviet rule among hundreds of thousands of Iranian subjects. The Soviet withdrawal, which seems to have been due partly to American pressure and partly to the hope (later proved to be mistaken) that they might get a firmer grip on Iran through the participation of communists in the central government in Teheran, was the only case since 1945 where Moscow has given up a territory in which a communist regime had been created. Six years later a new opportunity appeared, when the extreme nationalist government of Dr. Mosaddeq took power and was involved in bitter conflict with Britain in particular, and the West in general, on the question of nationalisation of oil. But Mosaddeq and the communists (the Tudeh Party) distrusted each other too much to combine forces. In August 1953 Mosaddeq was overthrown, and the communists (who had been banned in 1949 after an unsuccessful attempt to murder the Shah but had reappeared in the confusion of 1952) were once more driven underground. In the late

1950's, however, the Soviet propaganda offensive, and the activities of underground communists, were once more increased. Every effort was made not only to exploit the latent anti-Western nationalism and the discontent with social abuses and dictatorial rule, but also to convince the Iranian intelligentsia that the United States was the cause of all their sufferings, and that once Iran was neutral internal conditions would be better. The purpose of Soviet policy was easy to see. Iran must first be broken away from its alliance with the West, and then transformed from a neutral state into a satellite of the Soviet Union, in order that the Soviet Union might have direct access by land to the Arab world, and through the Arab world to Africa. When however in the late 1960's Soviet influence enormously increased in Egypt and other Arab countries, Iran became less important to Soviet policy. The Soviet government reduced its pressure, and indeed relations between the two countries became correct, with occasional expressions of official cordiality. Soviet policy concentrated on its work in the Arab countries. If these could be made solid satellites of the Soviet Union, then Iran's turn could be left until later.

In Iran's south-western neighbour, Iraq, the Soviet government appeared in 1958 to have won a decisive victory. Nuri es-Said and the dynasty were overthrown by army officers, but the communists quickly came out of hiding and organised a mass following in the urban proletariat of the cities. Their political influence grew so rapidly that it looked as if Iraq would soon become a 'people's democracy'. In the summer of 1959, however, they overreached themselves by their massacre of their opponents in Kirkuk. They were unable to mobilise the peasants under their leadership, and in the army General Kassem somehow maintained his authority. At the end of 1960 the communists had lost most of their influence. Thus, while the revolution of July 1958 was advantageous to Soviet policy by transforming Iraq from an ally of the West into a neutral, the Soviet government and the Iraqi communists by the end of 1960 had not succeeded in the further aim of bringing Iraq into the 'socialist camp'.

* * *

Castro's revolution in Cuba proved in the longer term to be an important, though limited, gain from the point of view of Soviet interests. Hatred against the dictatorship of Batista merged, at least in the minds of Castro and his closest colleagues, with hatred of the United States. The American government and public opinion were not at first hostile to Castro, who was well received on his first visit to the United States. But he himself, or his advisers, were determined on hostility to their northern neighbour. A series of deliberate attacks on American interests followed, and the fumbling counter-measures from Washington were exploited to create further hatred of 'Yankee imperialism'. The veterans of the civil war were increasingly replaced by Cuban communists, and experts from the Soviet bloc were called in. The fiasco of American-sponsored invasion by Cuban exiles in the 'Bay of Pigs' in 1961 drove Cuba further into the Soviet camp. The missiles crisis of October 1962 somewhat reduced Soviet prestige in Cuba. Nevertheless, Cuba remained the only communist regime in the Western Hemisphere, and continued to be economically subsidised by the Soviet government on a large scale. Geographical remoteness was of great advantage to Castro: he could take Soviet money, yet retain a certain independence of Soviet advice, even at times permitting himself the luxury of a few insults.

During the 1960's Soviet policy achieved some success in four newly independent African states—Algeria, Mali, Guinea and Ghana. All four were ruled by militant anti-Western groups, which professed devotion to 'African socialism', and did their best to propagate revolution throughout Africa. The Soviet leaders had some sympathy for their aims, or at least believed that they could make some use of their activities. At the same time, because these amateur international revolutionaries were not under reliable communist control, and were liable to provoke dangerous international complications, they were a source of potential embarrassment to the Soviet government. The overthrow of Ben Bella in Algeria was a set-back to Soviet influence, and in the following years Soviet policy appeared to be making Egypt rather than Algeria the centre of its influence in the Arab world. The overthrow of Nkrumah put an end to Soviet influence in Ghana, and serious friction occurred between Sékou Touré's government in Guinea and resident Soviet advisers.

The two major civil wars in Africa—between northern Arabic-speaking and southern Nilotics in Sudan, and between Ibos and the rest in Nigeria—also faced the Soviet leaders with awkward choices. In both cases they came down on the side of the strong against the weak, of the establishment against revolution. Just as the Americans appeared to see in Ojukwu and Biafra a black reincarnation of Jefferson Davis and the Confederacy, so the Soviet leaders seemed to see something rather like a Ukrainian separatist movement. In the Sudan, whatever sympathy they may have had for Nilotics exploited and massacred by the pale-skinned kinsmen of the Arab slave-traders of the past, was more than compensated by their calculation of the advantages to be derived from support of the Arab cause. In both cases Soviet policy, skilfully modelled on the conventional practices of nineteenth century European imperialist diplomacy, appeared in 1970 to have achieved success: in both Nigerian and Sudanese official circles the Soviet government was highly popular.

The principal aim held out by Soviet spokesmen to the leaders of independent neutralist states is 'economic independence'. Various conditions are necessary to achieve this aim. Foreign private capital must be confiscated, with little or no compensation. As long as any substantial foreign private concerns own property in such a country, or as long as foreign private capital plays an important part in any significant branch of the national economy, foreign business-men remain an invaluable scapegoat for nationalist and communist propaganda. Soviet and local communist spokesmen can and do deny that the country possesses economic independence until such survivals of 'imperialism' are wiped out.

Independent neutralist governments are also urged to refuse economic aid from Western governments. Much is made of the high proportion of Western aid which is spent either on defence or on economic needs which would not exist if there was not a vast burden of defence. American aid programmes, it is argued, are directly or indirectly controlled by the American monopoly capitalists: their aim is neither to defend nor to develop the countries which receive the aid, but to exploit them.

Trade with the West is also represented as a means of imperialist exploitation. The new states, it is argued, are forced to import a flood of unnecessary consumers' goods. These add to the luxury of the ruling classes, which are the effective agents of the Western imperialists, but do not benefit the economy at all. Moreover the price system is rigged to the advantage of the West: valuable exports of minerals and raw materials are underpriced, while imports of trash are overpriced.

In contrast to the dubious benefits of Western aid and trade are the marvellous prospects offered by the Soviet bloc. All Soviet transactions are described, by Soviet propagandists and by local communists, as 'generous help'. The same phrase was of course used *ad nauseam* in Eastern Europe, in the period of the forced price for Polish coal and the 'joint companies' described in a previous chapter, and is still used in a somewhat more restrained manner at the present time. All economic agreements with the West, wrote the eminent Soviet expert on Asian affairs, E. M. Zhukov in March 1959, 'must in fact always be of an unequal character and lead in the ultimate analysis to the renunciation of independence, subjection to the rule of foreign monopolies and surrender to foreign imperialism'. Another Soviet orientalist, V. Y. Avarin, interpreted the claim made by Western writers on economic problems in the underdeveloped societies, that Western private capital should be accepted 'in a climate which will secure adequate return to the investors and creditors', as a demand by the West that the new states should 'submit to unlimited exploitation by foreign capital and to unequal exchange' and should 'agree to restore the situation that prevailed ... before colonial oppression was overthrown'. The alternative to this bleak prospect is reliance on 'the unselfish disinterested aid of the socialist countries'. This has been already revealed in the ideal relationships existing within the 'socialist camp'. In the words of another Soviet writer, V. A. Fomina, 'the successful construction of socialism is possible precisely within the framework of the world socialist camp, on a basis of close mutual relations and co-operation, on the principles of full equality and respect for the integrity, state independence and sovereignty of the countries of socialism, and also of non-interference of one country or several countries in the affairs of others'. The events of November 1956 in Hungary never took place.

* * *

Soviet policy is designed both to increase trade and to offer aid, and special importance is given to winning over the 'national bourgeoisie'. This includes private businessmen of the Asian, African and Latin American nations; bureaucrats in their ministries and economic planning organisations; and independent members of the intellectual professions—the *intelligentsia*. The first of these three groups can best be won by developing a profitable trade. In this field Soviet policy has had some, though not yet very great, success. The second and third groups are much more impressed by Soviet contributions to the plans of industrial development. The bureaucrats are directly interested as their own livelihood is affected, while the intellectuals and students are inspired by the vision of national greatness to be based on industrial progress. Soviet aid is designed to strengthen the state sector of the economies of the new countries. Guarded approval is expressed by Soviet writers for the economic plans of India, the United

Arab Republic and other independent neutralist states. Zhukov may again be quoted: 'Given a comparatively low level of general economic and technological development in the East ... and given the economic diversity of these countries, the progressive tendency towards the transformation of the State (more correctly, the State-capitalist) sector of the economies of the non-socialist countries of the East into an important factor strengthening their economies and sovereignty should not be underrated'. And in practice since 1956 the Soviet Union has made substantial loans to India, Indonesia, Afghanistan, the U.A.R., Iraq, Ethiopia, Guinea and Cuba.

Soviet spokesmen have, however, left no doubt of their belief that Afro-Asian 'state capitalism' is not 'socialism', and that the 'national bourgeoisie' which is in power in these countries must in due course be replaced by the 'hegemony of the working class' (that is, by the dictatorship of communist parties). In the words of another eminent Soviet orientalist, A. A. Guber, 'We should not be misled by the adoption of programmes for "building a society of a socialist type", for the "building of socialism", by the socialist names taken by bourgeois parties, etc.' Another writer, V. V. Balabushevich, notes that the national bourgeoisie 'makes great efforts to discredit the communist parties in the workers' eyes ... using the slogans of socialism which have become so popular as a result of the enormous successes of the Soviet Union and the socialist countries. ... The achievement in several countries of State-capitalist measures, and the presence of elements of economic planning, are advanced as proof of development along a "socialist path" but one which takes account of "national peculiarities".' After independence has been won, 'a certain community of interests is preserved between the national bourgeoisie and the toiling masses in the cause of the defence of peace, the struggle against colonialism and the strengthening of political and economic independence, but at the same time the objective conditions arise for a further sharpening of the class struggle. In the fight for the strengthening of national independence, and for the most consistent solution of the tasks of the bourgeois-democratic revolution, the working class under the leadership of the communist and workers' parties has the possibility of attracting to its side the broad popular masses, and in the first instance the peasantry'. To quote Guber again, 'The working class . . . has regarded the gaining of national independence merely as a stage, a necessary requisite for social change and the subsequent growing over of the national colonial revolution into a socialist revolution. The national bourgeoisie saw in national independence the attainment of its ultimate aim . . . undivided rule in a sovereign state'.

In other words, the claim of the Nehru dynasty, Nasser and others to be socialists is fraudulent. Socialism is inevitable, but it will come only when the communist parties have seized power, and have made short shrift of the 'national bourgeoisie', as the Chinese communists did in the famous 'three anti' and 'five anti' campaigns of 1952. Then only will 'national independence' be truly 'strengthened', by the removal of any influence inhibiting the beneficent influences of the 'socialist camp'. Then only will the new states enjoy the blissful degree of independence, based on 'the principles of full equality and respect for the integrity, state independence and sovereignty of the countries of socialism, and also of non-interference of one country or several countries in the affairs of others', which is the lot of the Hungarians and their happy neighbours.

* * *

During the 1950's it became obvious to the outside world that there was serious friction between the Soviet and Chinese communist leaders, and during the 1960's the quarrel became public and grew more bitter, culminating in large-scale frontier battles in 1969.

The origins and causes of the quarrel can only be briefly summarised here. The events of 1927, and Stalin's disastrous directives to the Chinese communists, had left a bitter memory among the Chinese party veterans. This had been aggravated by the long protracted preference of Stalin for other communist leaders rather than for Mao Tse-tung, even when the latter had in practice proved himself outstanding in ability and popularity. Stalin's maintenance of diplomatic relations with the government of Chiang Kai-shek right up to the end of the Chinese Civil War also must have annoyed Mao considerably. Once the communists were in control of China, they found the Soviet government extremely unwilling to give them anything like the amount of economic aid which their country needed, and to which they felt they were entitled in view of their services to the revolutionary cause. They especially resented Soviet refusal to supply them with atomic weapons. The cult of Stalin in the Soviet Union conflicted with the cult of Mao in China: neither side was willing to recognise the idol of the other as the equal of its own. When Stalin died, the claims made for Mao increased, and the Chinese clearly showed that they regarded the successors to Stalin as a lesser breed. In 1958 the Chinese party put forward the extraordinary ideological claim that it was approaching the stage of establishing communism (whereas the Soviet leaders, whose party had been in power for forty years, admitted that they were still far from this stage). The claim was watered down in an official Chinese statement at the end of 1958, but it had undoubtedly created rage in Moscow. In the next years the Chinese leaders were infuriated by Soviet refusal to back China effectively against the United States in regard to Formosa, by Khrushchov's visit to Eisenhower, and by Soviet support to India. By 1960 the fact of hostility had become far more important than its original causes. Something must be said of the nature and consequences of Soviet-Chinese hostility.

Ideological rivalry between the Soviet and Chinese leaders had an impact on the relations of both governments to other communist parties and to other countries. The impact in Eastern Europe has already been mentioned. In Western Europe the communist parties supported the Soviet Union: the vested interests of their *apparat* were obvious, and only small groups preferred Mao.[1] In the Far East the communist parties, especially those of India and Japan, were seriously divided or disrupted. In South-East Asia the Soviet government was obliged to strike a revolutionary posture, in order not to be thought less militant than China.

In Vietnam both governments continued to give aid to the communists: the Soviet Union was able to provide modern weapons of better quality, but the guerrilla know-how and the general political influence of the Chinese should not be underrated. There was some tendency in the United States in the late 1960's to believe that the Soviet leaders wished to end the Vietnam war by a compromise; were willing to help the United States towards such a compromise provided that it was mainly favourable to the North Vietnamese and the Vietcong; and were embarrassed by the uncompromising demagogy of the Chinese, which limited their freedom of action. In fact these beliefs were based on inadequate evidence: it was equally likely that the Soviet leaders wished the war to continue indefinitely. Far more important to Brezhnev and his colleagues than the terms desired by the North Vietnamese was the fact that the Vietnam war was demoralising American political and social life and poisoning the relations of the United States with many of its allies in Europe and Asia. Thus in the case of Vietnam, though mutual suspicion between the Russians and Chinese was profound, it may be argued that the common interests between the two governments were stronger than the points of conflict.

This was clearly not the case in Indonesia. Here in the early 1960's the Communist Party, its numbers enormously swollen and its prestige high, was under Chinese influence, while the Soviet government, as the main source of weapons, had a predominant influence on the Indonesian armed forces. However, the communists overreached themselves,

[1] I am here speaking of small groups of communist party members. There were of course in many West European countries other groups, chiefly of young people and students, who professed devotion to Mao's teaching, but these were not members of the official communist parties.

and President Sukarno with them, and in 1965 a military dictatorship came to power which suppressed the communists. In the subsequent repression many thousands of communists were massacred, and not only China but also the Soviet Union lost its influence on Indonesian politics. As the Soviet leaders saw it, the adventurism of the Chinese had led to a disaster for the communist cause.

In South America too Soviet and Chinese interests have been directly opposed. The Soviet government has discouraged communist parties from guerrilla action, and has encouraged the formation of political alliances, and if possible governments, which include bourgeois politicians and army officers, provided only that they are nationalist and strongly anti-North American. The Chinese extol the virtues of guerrilla warfare. In tropical Africa the same difference exists, though the Soviet government is not so strongly opposed to guerrilla action as in Latin America. In Tanzania and in the revolutionary movements of the southern African countries, the supporters of the Soviet Union and of China view one another with suspicion, though perhaps here, as in Indo-China, the common interests outweigh the differences.

The conflict between the Soviet Union and China is not however only ideological: it is also a clash between states, and indeed between empires. The Far Eastern provinces of Russia were acquired in 1860 by the Treaty of Peking, far the most onerous in terms of territory sacrificed of all the 'unequal treaties' forced on China in the age of triumphant European imperialism. This has been frequently pointed out by Chinese communist spokesmen during the 1960's. It is true that the Chinese have not asked for restitution of the territories, but only for an admission by the Soviet leaders of the unequivocally imperialist character of the acquisition of these Russian provinces. The Soviet leaders have not given this admission. Behind this academic and dogmatic argument there may or may not lie a Chinese desire to recover the provinces. One may however be sure that the Soviet leaders fear that such a desire exists. There is also evidence that the Soviet public are genuinely alarmed about Chinese territorial aims, and the bogey of the swarming hundreds of millions of little yellow men threatening the Russian fatherland is causing much more widespread alarm than in the days of the Tsars. Another source of dispute is Mongolia. Both Kuomintang and communists were long reluctant to recognise as an independent state this former tributary of the Chinese Empire. The communists did in the end recognise Mongolia, but this did not end the conflict of interests: it merely meant that the struggle for influence between Russians and Chinese would continue within the independent republic. Chinese Turkestan, or Sinkiang, is yet another object of rivalry. The population of this province, as of the neighbouring Central Asian republics of the Soviet Union, is mainly neither Russian nor Chinese, but consists of various Moslem peoples of Turkic or Iranian language. These peoples have little reason to prefer the Chinese to the Russians, but every reason to try to benefit from the quarrel between the two giants, in order to gain advantages for themselves. Like the governments and the communist parties of Eastern Europe, those of Mongolia and of the Central Asian Soviet republics may be expected to increase their demands in the next years, and this in turn is likely to increase mutual suspicion between Russia and China and tension throughout Central Asia.

One of the most alarming developments for the Soviet Union in the 1960's was the increasing friendship between China and Pakistan. Should a major Moslem state, with large populations of Turkic and Iranian speech, become closely associated with China, the force of attraction of this combination on Soviet Moslems might be considerable. Until this time the Soviet leaders, while professing friendship for India, had treated Pakistan with contempt, as a mere invention of the British imperialists and satellite of the Americans. As the conflict between China and India grew, and especially after the large-scale fighting in 1962 on the north-east frontier, Soviet attitudes began to change. In 1965, after the outbreak of fighting between India and

Pakistan, the Soviet government came forward as a mediator. The Indian government, which had previously always bitterly resented the efforts of mediation of Western Powers, agreed to meet the Pakistan leaders in Tashkent. No solution to the quarrel was found, and from the Indian point of view, Soviet policy was now less favourable than it had been, since it now recognised India and Pakistan as equals instead of exclusively accepting the Indian case. However, after Mrs. Gandhi became Premier, Indian spokesmen were ever more generous in their statements of gratitude to the Soviet Union, while keeping up the old flow of moral denunciation of the Americans and their European friends. Economic aid from the Soviet Union to India was a small fraction of American aid, but in the supply of arms the Soviet Union took first place. Needing the internal support of the pro-Soviet communist party (as opposed to the two other, more revolutionary, communist parties with which the Indian political scene was blessed), and hoping for Soviet military support against China, Mrs. Gandhi's government increasingly wooed the Soviet government and insulted those whom Moscow disliked. However, it would be wrong to consider India a Soviet satellite. A far more apt historical parallel would be nineteenth-century Persia. The British and Russian ambassadors in Teheran in Victorian times between them dominated nominally sovereign Persia. Sometimes the two Great Powers co-operated with each other, whether at the expense of the Persians or (as they at least fancied) to their advantage; more often they intrigued against each other; always they distrusted each other. In the 1960's India became jointly dependent on the United States and the Soviet Union, increasingly at their mercy. The policies of the Soviet Union and the United States in India were basically antagonistic to each other, but there was, at least on the American side, a certain belief that the two Powers had a common interest in maintaining India as an independent state and in strengthening its economy and its military forces. Thus, twenty years after it had proudly achieved its independence, India appeared to be relapsing into the status of a semi-colonial dependency paralysed by its economic inefficiency, corruption and mutually incompatible linguistic nationalisms; at the mercy of the two world powers; great only in its output of moralising rhetoric. The Soviet Union appeared to be achieving in India a position more powerful than the Tsars had dreamed of: whether this would be a source of strength to the Soviet Union, or would merely cause Russian resources to be poured down a bottomless drain, it was too early to predict.

Another region in which the Soviet leaders followed in the footsteps of the Tsars, and achieved greater success, was the Middle East. Substantial Soviet penetration into the Arab world began with the military aid to Egypt in 1955 which set in motion the events (refusal of American aid to the Assuan Dam, nationalisation of the Suez Canal by Egypt and protracted indecision by the American Secretary of State John Foster Dulles) which culminated in the abortive Anglo-French invasion of Egypt in November 1956. After the Anglo-French defeat, Soviet prestige rapidly rose in the Arab countries. During the following years Soviet influence in Iraq, Syria, Egypt and Algeria rose and fell in connection both with the vagaries of American policy and with successive palace revolutions and battles between warring Arab cliques, but the long-term trend was towards Soviet supremacy. The outbreak of the Arab-Israeli war of 1967 owed much to Soviet advice and to Soviet influence at the United Nations. The war was a military disaster for the Arabs, but it did not cause a setback to Soviet influence. The determination of the Arab extremists for revenge at any cost, and the fear of the extremists which held all Arab governments in thrall, ensured that the governments would follow any Soviet lead which seemed likely to assist their aims. But if Arab willingness to accept satellite status to Russia was not in doubt, Soviet willingness to back the Arabs was much less clear. The leaders of a world power, with interests in many other lands and with much to lose from war, were bound to use caution. In this they resembled their predecessors the Tsars.

The Soviet leaders themselves would of course fiercely deny that their policy in the Middle East was imperialistic: on the contrary, it was inspired by the disinterested desire to rescue the Arab peoples from Western imperialism and its Israeli agents. It is of course arguable that Israel is an imperialist state. It is a fact that Israel was established by driving hundreds of thousands of Palestinian Arabs from their homes (whether the expulsion of these Arabs, and the miserable conditions in which they have lived for a quarter of a century, is as much the fault of the governments of Arab states as of the Israelis, is another question). It should not however be forgotten that the Soviet Union supported the creation of Israel in 1948. More important is the question of Soviet motivation in 1970. Soviet influence in the Arab countries has led to a large increase in the Soviet naval presence in the Mediterranean, to the appearance of Soviet warships in the Indian Ocean, to an agreement with Mauritius which may lead to the placing of important facilities at the disposal of Soviet naval forces, and to an obviously growing urgency in the Soviet desire to have the Suez Canal working again—this time as a Soviet-controlled waterway, in the same sense in which the Panama Canal is an American-controlled waterway. The drive to control the southern shore of the Mediterranean, and as much as possible of the eastern shore of Africa and the southern shore of Asia may of course be inspired by disinterested passion for humanity, for whom are intended the blessings of revolutions to be carried out by local revolutionaries with a little purely disinterested aid from high-minded Soviet advisers. But if set against the Russian historical background, it looks remarkably like a continuation of the imperialism of the Tsars, by not very different means but with greater single-mindedness and efficiency.

7

The New Imperialism

THE Soviet Union is an imperialist Power in three senses.
The Soviet government has inherited from the Russian
Empire about ninety million subjects, divided into a large
number of small and medium-sized nations, to whom it
denies, more ruthlessly than the Tsars denied, the right to
choose national independence. Secondly, it rules indirectly
a further ninety million in Eastern Europe, divided into
seven nations, whose territory the Soviet Army occupied
in 1944–1945, and a further 14 million in Mongolia and
North Korea. Thirdly, the Communist Party of the Soviet
Union, inspired by a missionary ideology, seeks by a variety
of weapons and tactics to impose its doctrines and its
institutions on the other nations of the world.

The Soviet communists utterly deny that they are imperialists. On the contrary, they claim to be the leaders of the
world-wide movement against imperialism. 'The imperialists' is a phrase reserved exclusively for the United States
and its allies. According to the Soviet version of history,
the non-Russian peoples chose voluntarily to remain within
Soviet Russia in the years after 1917. The Soviet army
entered Mongolia, Azerbaidjan, Georgia, the Baltic republics and eastern Poland in response to the wishes of the
peoples of those lands for 'liberation'. In Eastern Europe
after 1944 'the toiling masses', headed by the communist
parties, overthrew the reactionaries supported by the
United States. In so far as the Soviet armed forces contributed to their victory, this was but a generous brotherly
gesture in response to the wishes of the peoples. In November 1956 the Soviet army gave generous disinterested aid to
the 'worker-peasant government' of János Kádár in its task

of liberating Hungary from the fascist and reactionary gangs subsidised by the Americans. Soviet intervention in Czechoslovakia in 1968 was also a case of friendly help given in defence of socialism. In so far as the Soviet government works for the cause of communism, it is merely helping the inevitable progress of history.

This view is based on certain assumptions which it is worth stating explicitly.

Firstly, the Marxist doctrine of the ineluctable progress of human societies through revolution to socialism, and the messianic role of the working class in this process, are taken as established truths.

Secondly, *the* party of the working class is the Communist Party of the Soviet Union. In November 1917 the Bolshevik Party led by Lenin seized power, with the support of a large part of the working class of Petrograd. It follows from this, not only that the party represented the aspirations of the workers at that time (which most historians would probably admit), but that it embodied for all time the immanent interests of the working class, first in Russia and then in all other countries in which parties, based on the Bolshevik model, were subsequently created. The decisive factor is that communist parties consist of persons who are in possession of the truly proletarian theory, the science of Marxism-Leninism. Whether the flesh-and-blood workers in a given country support its communist party is a secondary consideration. Whether they know or admit it or not, their immanent interests are represented and defended by the communist party.

Thirdly, the will of the party, which reflects the will of the working class, is expressed by its leaders, who are always right as long as they are leaders. In the history of the party 'mistakes' have been committed (such as the wrongful arrest of millions, and the wrongful execution of hundreds of thousands of party members in the Great Purge of 1936–1938), but the party was never wrong. The 'party line', as formulated by its leaders and carried out by its apparatus, has always been right. It is indeed right because it is the party line. The excesses of the period of 'the cult of personality' (the last years of the autocracy of Stalin) were regrettable. They were indeed bitterly denounced by no less authoritative a person than Stalin's successor Khrushchov. But they did not in any way diminish the historical infallibility of the party leadership.

It follows from this that it is inconceivable that the leaders of a communist party could be guilty of imperialism. Direct or indirect conquest of any country by the Communist Party of the Soviet Union can only be liberation, and can only lead to the establishment of true liberty and social justice. Liberty and social justice are indeed, by definition, what the leaders of the Soviet Communist Party, representing the will of the party, which represents the will of the working class, say they are.

* * *

Those who cannot accept these assumptions may conclude that Soviet domination over the non-Russian peoples of the Soviet Union and over the satellite peoples of Europe and Asia is imperialism, and that world-wide communist aims of expansion are imperialist. But this need not mean a wholesale moral condemnation of the Soviet record. In the present author's view the Soviet record has both good and bad points. In his opinion, 'imperialism' is in any case not an unmitigated evil. British imperialism in Africa, for example, has undoubtedly brought evil, in the form of many acts of injustice, and especially in the humiliation of the most educated and westernised elements in the social structures of the African peoples. At the same time it has undoubtedly brought great benefits. This is admitted by many of the peoples formerly belonging to the British Empire, especially perhaps by Indians, Pakistanis, Malays and Nigerians. Equally the Soviet empire has brought violence and cruelty, but has also brought progress and opportunity.

Some of the benefits of Soviet rule date from Imperial Russian times. Public law and administration were certainly better in Russian Turkestan than under the traditional rulers of Samarkand or Kokand. The land reform carried out by General Kaufmann was a great act of social justice. Development of cotton farming in Turkestan was begun under the Tsars. In the Soviet period, economic development was pushed much further and faster. New industries were created in the regions of non-Russian population. Vast progress was made in education at all levels, from the village school to the university. In this field there is only one example in history which can stand comparison with the Soviet achievement—that of Japan in the Meiji era.

It may indeed be argued that the material achievement of the Soviet regime is greater than that of the British Empire. But two points should here be made. The first is that the non-Russian peoples of the Russian Empire were very much more advanced in their general level of civilisation than the peoples of the British colonies in Africa, and even than those of India. The second is that the proportion of the metropolitan to the colonial peoples was quite different. The proportion of Russians to all non-Russians was about 1 : 1, and of Russians to Central Asian Moslems about 5 : 1, whereas the proportion of British to Asian and African colonial subjects was about 1 : 10.

But a more important reason for the less striking material progress of the British colonies was the different attitude taken by the British rulers towards the beliefs, traditions and institutions of the colonial peoples. British governments and administrators were usually inclined to respect the existing social hierarchies and cultures, and were unwilling to force British ideas or customs on them. There were of course great differences between regions and periods. After the Indian Mutiny of 1857 the reluctance to interfere with local institutions was increased. It may be argued that British rule artificially prolonged archaic habits of mind, and that in some parts of Africa the doctrine of 'indirect rule' gave too much importance to reactionary chiefs, or even created artificial chieftaincies where these had no solid foundation. But reluctance to force the conqueror's values on the conquered is not necessarily ignoble, and tolerance for other habits and faiths is a part of the theory and practice of liberal democracy. The Soviet rulers had no such inhibitions. They believed that they knew exactly what was good for the Ukrainians, Georgians, Uzbeks, Yakuts, Poles, Roumanians and the rest, and nothing was going to stop them from bringing these benefits to these fortunate people. If executions, deportations and mass famine were needed, then they should be used.

*　　*　　*

Asian and African intellectuals no doubt vary in their views as to the relative sins of Western and Soviet imperialism. They know much more about the first than the second. Some may argue that economic progress and mass education are so important that it is worth paying the price of totalitarianism and of subjection to communist parties whose policies are essentially dictated from Moscow. Others may believe that communist parties are quite free from Moscow's control. Very few Asians or Africans living outside the Soviet bloc have any personal knowledge of what it means to be ruled by a communist party. Very few have spoken to Asians who do live under communist rule, and most of those to whom they have spoken have been official representatives of the communist party, such as N. A. Mukhitdinov, a former member of the CPSU Presidium. It is no easier for a visiting Indian or Egyptian than for a visiting Englishman or Frenchman to discover what are the inmost feelings of an Uzbek collective farmer or an Azerbaidjani worker.

But Asian and African nationalists outside the Soviet bloc frequently and sincerely declare that economic progress handed to them by foreign masters is not enough, that they want above all independence and freedom for their peoples, freedom to decide what kind of economic development they want. If Sir Roy Welensky's arguments (based on plenty of solid facts) about the economic benefits of the Federation for Africans did not convince the Rhodesian African *intelligentsia*, one may doubt whether the essentially similar arguments of the Soviet communist leaders convince educated Uzbeks or Azerbaidjanis. But whereas Mr. Kaunda and Mr. Nkomo and Dr. Banda could and did express their opposition to Welensky's policies, no Azerbaidjani or Uzbek dare express a desire that his country should be independent, and no leader of a communist party in Eastern Europe dare suggest that his country should secede from its alliance with the Soviet Union. Imre Nagy did just that, and his fate is not forgotten.

The journey to 'socialism' of the Soviet type is a one-way trip: there is no return ticket.

* * *

The Soviet plans for the expansion of communism are at present directed mainly against the underdeveloped societies. The manipulation of nationalism offers great opportunities. The possibilities of linguistic nationalism in India and in tropical Africa are enormous. Systematic exploitation of race hatred, at the United Nations and elsewhere, may lose the Soviet leaders sympathy in some quarters, but it is likely to win them sympathy in others, and among minorities in independent states as well as from nationalist movements in colonies.

Whether Soviet expansion will secure great victories in the next decades depends partly on the resistance it meets and partly on the vigour with which it is pursued.

Resistance is impossible unless there is in the world a centre of military power which can counterbalance Soviet power. This is at present provided by the United States. If it did not exist, none of the neutral states that border the Soviet Union and China could hope to preserve their freedom. That these states should prefer not to ally themselves with the United States, but to enjoy the security offered by American strength without contributing to it, is perfectly understandable from the point of view of their national interests. Other states, however, have decided to take on themselves some part of the burden. If none were willing to accept the obligations of alliance, the centre of power itself might prove inadequate to maintain the present uneasy balance of terror. This is of course the aim of Soviet policy, which seeks to convert America's allies into neutrals, and neutrals into satellites of the Soviet bloc.

But military power is only a part of the resistance to communist expansion. The new imperialism can be withstood only by combining military strength with political and social action, with economic and educational policies which cannot be discussed in the present short work.

* * *

The second main factor—the vigour with which the new imperialism is pursued—depends on the internal development of Soviet society and on the relations between the Soviet Union and China. These too are vast subjects which far exceed the scope of the present work. A general observation may, however, be made.

The Victorian masters of the nineteenth century British Empire were a ruling class which was derived partly from the semi-aristocratic, semi-commercial founders of British India in the previous century and partly from the new bourgeoisie created by the industrial revolution. These men had high moral and political ideals, and believed that they were putting them into practice in the Empire. They ruled with complete self-confidence. Later generations, developing the same moral and political ideals, saw that they conflicted with the facts of imperial domination over other nations, whose new leaders seized on the ideals and used them against their masters. The masters' conscience grew uneasy, their self-confidence withered away, and the elite abdicated.

The founders of the Russian Empire may be compared with the eighteenth-century founders of the British. After the collapse of the Imperial regime, the vast country, Russian and non-Russian areas alike, was ruled for about ten years by a combination of revolutionary *intelligentsia* and the surviving lower levels of the old regime's bureaucracy. But in the 1930's the forced industrial revolution created (as the earlier unplanned industrial revolutions in the West had created) a vast new upper stratum of managers and technicians and experts. In the 1970's these are the administrators of the Soviet Union, the equivalent of the business-men, civil servants and free professions of Western society. They are the Soviet *state bourgeoisie*, different in many respects from the capitalist *private bourgeoisie* of the West, yet in many respects resembling it. The Victorian outlook, in private morals and aesthetic taste, of this *state bourgeoisie*, has often been pointed out. Perhaps a more important similarity is their self-confidence and self-righteousness, their conviction that they know what is best for their people and for other people, their determination to maintain their own rule with an iron hand and to extend it to others. The arguments of Soviet historians that the conquest of Central Asia by the Tsars was objectively progressive are essentially a Marxist-Leninist version of the arguments of Kipling.

It is clear that the connection between the rise of new classes to power and the growth of a brash and self-righteous nationalism, which is visible in the history of so many modern nations, is no less applicable to Soviet society. Soviet spokesmen insist that the virtues of their socialist society exclude the sins of earlier societies. But the sad truth is that Soviet society possesses no mysterious essence guaranteeing it from sin: on the contrary, the belief in its peculiar virtues is in fact an example of the sin of self-righteousness produced by a type of social transformation which is common to the Soviet Union in the twentieth century and European and North American societies in the nineteenth.

The interesting question presents itself, whether the evolution from self-righteousness to self-questioning, from the ruthless exercise of power to the abdication of the elite, which has taken place in the last half-century in Britain and France, will repeat itself in the Soviet Union.

If it does, who will be the gainer—the peoples of Europe, Asia and Africa, spared from the danger of Soviet imperialism, or the younger, brasher and still more self-righteous imperialism of China?

Already at the end of the 1960's there were some signs of bad conscience in the Soviet upper stratum. As in nineteenth century Russia, and as in Victorian Britain, the first protests came from a few intellectuals, such brave men as Pavel Litvinov and Academician Sakharov. More surprising was the protest of General Peter Grigorenko at the injustice done to the Crimean Tatars. Whereas most of the nations deported during the Second World War were declared innocent in the Khrushchov era, and allowed in principle (not always in practice) to return to their homelands, this permission was not given to the Crimean Tatars. That a Russian general should speak out on behalf of a non-Russian people was something new and deeply encouraging. The Crimean Tatars also spoke out on their own behalf, and several were condemned to prison by Soviet courts in consequence.

These, then, were hopeful signs, and the rapidity of social, political and international change in the third quarter of the twentieth century were such as to make all prediction valueless. Nevertheless, it must be said that in 1970 there was still no sign of the abdication of power by the political elite of the Soviet Union in the narrowest sense—the leadership of the CPSU. The vigour and ruthlessness of the new imperialism still seemed undiminished.

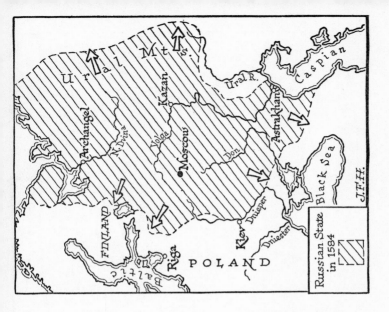

Russian State
in 1584

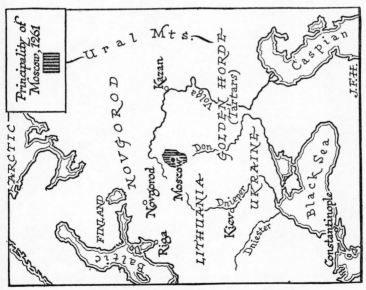

Principality of
Moscow, 1261

The Growth of the Russian Empire
1 and 2

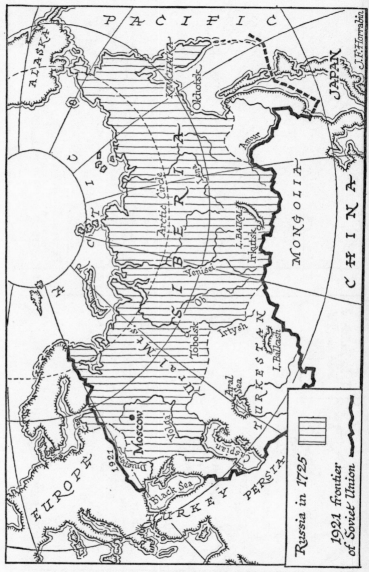

The Growth of the Russian Empire

3

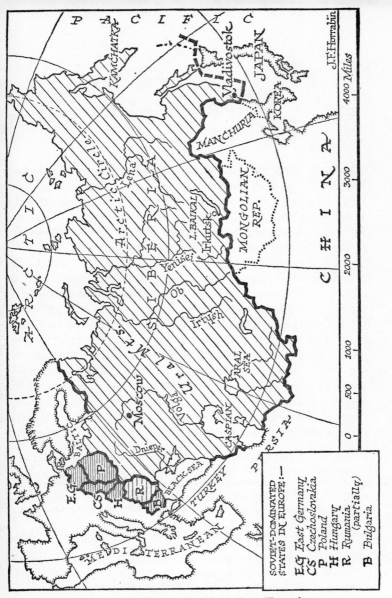

The Growth of the Russian Empire

4

Short Reading List

THE published sources for the present work are mostly in Russian or in East European languages. The sources for Chapter 6 are almost exclusively to be found in specialised Russian periodicals. Of these I must mention *Sovetskoe Vostokovedenie* (and its successor *Problemy Vostokovedenia*); *Sovetskaya Etnografia*; and *Sovremenny Vostok*. The first two maintain a fairly high level of scholarship, but the third is essentially a propaganda publication. Valuable statements of communist policy towards the underdeveloped societies may also be found in the international communist journal, the title of whose English edition is *World Marxist Review*.

As it is assumed that most readers of the present work cannot read Russian or East European languages, the following short list is confined to works in English or French. Those readers, however, who can read Russian will find ample bibliographies in these works. Those who can read German may be advised also to consult the excellent periodical *Osteuropa*, published since the war in Stuttgart.

Bennigsen, A., and Quelquejay, C., *Les mouvements nationaux chez les musulmans de Russie*, Paris 1960

Carr, E. H., *The Bolshevik Revolution* (Vol. 1, Part III), London 1950

Fejtö, François, *Histoire des démocraties populaires*, Paris 1952

Kautsky, J. H., *Moscow and the Communist Party of India*, New York 1956

Kazemzadeh, F., *The Struggle for Transcaucasia (1917–1921)*, New York 1951

Kolarz, W., *Russia and her Colonies*, London 1952; *The Peoples of the Soviet Far East*, London 1954

Lenin, V. I., *Imperialism* (easily accessible in many editions)

Pierce, R. A., *Russian Central Asia 1867–1917*, Berkeley (California) 1960

Pipes, R., *The Formation of the Soviet Union*, Cambridge (Massachusetts) 1954

Reshetar, J. S., *The Ukrainian Revolution*, Princeton 1952

Seton-Watson, Hugh, *The East European Revolution*, London 1950

Strachey, John, *The End of Empire*, London 1959

Vakar, N. P., *Belorussia: the Making of a Nation*, Cambridge (Massachusetts) 1956

Wheeler, Geoffrey, *Racial Problems in Soviet Muslim Asia*, London 1960

Zenkovsky, S. A., *Pan-Turkism and Islam in Russia*, Cambridge (Massachusetts) 1960

The work by Bennigsen and Quelquejay is an excellent study of the Tatar movement, with special reference to the activities of Sultan-Galiev. The work by Kautsky is concerned not only with India but with communist attitudes to free Asia as a whole in the last years of Stalin's life. It is the best published analysis of the subject known to me.

Index

Ugn
DK
63.3
S35
1971

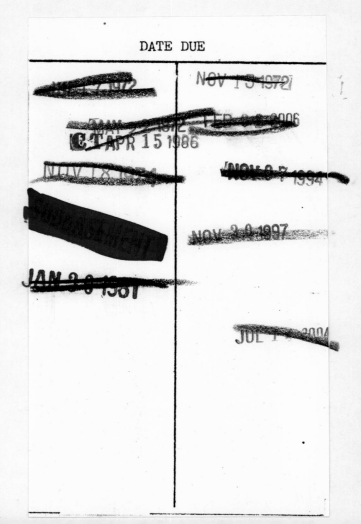